Modern John Buchan

Modern John Buchan:
A Critical Introduction

By

Nathan Waddell

CAMBRIDGE
SCHOLARS

P U B L I S H I N G

Modern John Buchan: A Critical Introduction, by Nathan Waddell

This book first published 2009

Cambridge Scholars Publishing

12 Back Chapman Street, Newcastle upon Tyne, NE6 2XX, UK

British Library Cataloguing in Publication Data
A catalogue record for this book is available from the British Library

ISBN (10): 1-4438-1370-2, ISBN (13): 978-1-4438-1370-9

TABLE OF CONTENTS

ACKNOWLEDGEMENTS

First books incur many debts. First and foremost, I would like to thank Andrzej Gasiorek, whose critical commentary has improved this text in any number of ways. Without his encouragement, intellectual support, and friendship I would not have made it to the finish line. Deborah Parsons suggested I write a book on Buchan to begin with. My thanks to her for assorted references and backing, and for starting me off on what eventually became a surprisingly enjoyable writing experience. Kate Macdonald (University of Ghent, Belgium) has been a valuable source of constructive criticism as my ideas have developed. Thank you to Kate, Andrew Lownie, and Scott Klein (of Wake Forest University, USA) for reading the book in draft manuscript. Roger Luckhurst (Birkbeck, University of London) read a couple of chapters and made many helpful suggestions. At Cambridge Scholars, thanks to Amanda Millar, to Carol Koulikourdi for her contract management, and to Andy Nercessian for commissioning the book in the first place. Thanks to Charles Reeve-Tucker and Anna Jamson, both of whom read parts of the book at various stages. Continuing thanks to Christopher Gee for over fifteen years of close friendship, silliness, and what can only be described as brotherhood. Thanks to Phil Peters, Esha Khanna, James Ward, Simon Bartlett, Lucy Dagger, and James Wilkins for several years of laughter and learning. General thanks to the wonderfully kind Charles and Jennifer Reeve-Tucker, and to the Waddell, Horsfall, Reeve-Tucker, and Macgregor clans more generally. If all were tangentially involved in this project, that involvement was vital to it anyhow. I wish my nan (Joan Horsfall) and granddad (Eric Waddell) had lived long enough to read it.

Mum and dad: this is for you, with much love, appreciation, and sympathy. It's also for Alice, who means more to me than I can say.

Parts of Chapters Two and Three first appeared in a slightly different form in my chapter for Kate Macdonald, ed., *Reassessing John Buchan: Beyond The Thirty-Nine Steps* (Pickering and Chatto, 2009), and parts of the "Conclusion" first appeared in *The Birmingham Journal of Literature and Language*. My thanks to Paul Lee and Laura Hilton, of Pickering and Chatto and previously of the *Journal*, for their kind permission to reprint these materials here.

ABBREVIATIONS

Where possible, all references to Buchan's works are to the Oxford World's Classics edition (David Daniell, general ed. (Oxford: Oxford University Press, 1993-6)). Italics are as in the original source, unless stated otherwise.

AC	*The African Colony: Studies in the Reconstruction* (William Blackwood, 1903)
CC	*Comments and Characters* (Nelson, 1940)
CG	*Castle Gay* (1930) (House of Stratus, 2001)
CM	*The Courts of the Morning* (1929) (B & W, 1993)
CO	*Canadian Occasions* (Hodder, 1940)
G	*Greenmantle* (1916) (OUP, 1993)
H	*Huntingtower* (1922) (OUP, 1996)
HR	*Homilies and Recreations* (Nelson, 1926)
KG	*The King's Grace* (University of London Press, 1935)
LL	*A Lost Lady of Old Years* (1899) (B & W, 1995)
LW	*A Lodge in the Wilderness* (Nelson, 1906)
MD	*Men and Deeds* (Peter Davies, 1935)
MHD	*Memory Hold-the-Door* (Hodder, 1940)
MS	*Mr Standfast* (1919) (OUP, 1993)
NFT	*The Novel and the Fairy Tale* (English Association, 1931)
OC	*Oliver Cromwell* (1934) (Sphere, 1970)
PH	*The Power-House* (1913/1916) (House of Stratus, 2003)
PJ	*Prester John* (1910) (OUP, 1994)
SEB	*Some Eighteenth-Century Byways* (Blackwood, 1908)
SHR	*Sick Heart River* (1941) (OUP, 1994)
TH	*The Three Hostages* (1924) (OUP, 1995)
TNS	*The Thirty-Nine Steps* (1915) (OUP, 1993)
WW	*Witch Wood* (1927) (OUP, 1993)

Adam Smith, *JB*
    Janet Adam Smith, *John Buchan: A Biography* (1965) (OUP, 85)
Lownie, *PC*
    Andrew Lownie, *The Presbyterian Cavalier* (1995) (Pimlico, 2002)
Macdonald, *CMF*
    Kate Macdonald, *A Companion to the Mystery Fiction* (Jefferson, NC:
    McFarland, 2009)
Macdonald, *RJB*
    Kate Macdonald, ed., *Reassessing John Buchan: Beyond* The Thirty-
    Nine Steps (Pickering & Chatto, 2009)

All references to Buchan's short stories are to the Thistle edition (Andrew
Lownie, ed. (1996-7)):

SS1   *The Complete Short Stories*, Vol. 1 (1996)
SS2   *The Complete Short Stories*, Vol. 2 (1997)
SS3   *The Complete Short Stories*, Vol. 3 (1997)

CHAPTER ONE

INTRODUCTION

In a commendatory account entitled *The "Wreath'd Trellis"* (1955) William Buchan writes of his father:

> There are many different ways in which people write; my father's way was just one, but possibly not the most usual. He never, to my knowledge, ever burnt any midnight oil. He wrote in prescribed hours of work. He worked from nine till one and between five and seven in the evening. He never worked in the afternoon, and all his life he never struck a tap of work after dinner.[1]

This compressed schedule produced a massive body of literary and non-literary work. John Buchan wrote over twenty-five novels, over fifty short stories, a twenty-four volume history of the Great War written as it was unfolding, over ten biographical studies, poetry, assorted military and historical chronicles, and more besides. All of this was churned out while Buchan worked at full tilt in a variety of literary and non-literary contexts, among them journalism, propaganda work, war reportage, editing, and the civil service. He was also a husband, and a father to one daughter and three sons.

Buchan was born in Perth in 1875, and attended Glasgow University and Brasenose College, Oxford. Raised as a Calvinist, in 1901 he was called to the Bar in London, much like Thomas Carlyle Craw in his novel *Castle Gay* (1930), who went to the capital "according to the secular fashion of ambitious Scottish youth" (*CG* 20). Unlike Craw, Buchan's education was certainly distinguished. He achieved a First Class Honours degree at Oxford, and in addition to the Stanhope he won the Bridgeman and Newdigate prizes as well (Lownie, *PC* 62). After working as Alfred Milner's private secretary in South Africa between 1901 and 1903, in 1907 Buchan joined the publishing house Thomas Nelson and Sons, an

---

[1] William Buchan, *The "Wreath'd Trellis": John Buchan the Writer by His Son* (1955) (Special Collections, Douglas Library, Queen's University at Kingston, 1985), 12.

association that would last for over twenty years. During the First World War he worked as a war correspondent and wrote two of his best-known novels, *The Thirty-Nine Steps* (1915) and *Greenmantle* (1916). By 1935 he had been made a Deputy-Chairman of Reuters, a Member of Parliament for the Scottish Universities, a Companion of Honour, and Lord High Commissioner to the General Assembly of the Church of Scotland. In 1935 Buchan was appointed Governor-General of Canada and appointed Lord Tweedsmuir of Elsfield, after the parish near Oxford where Buchan had been living since 1919. In 1937 Buchan was elected as Chancellor of Edinburgh University and made a Privy Councillor. He died in February 1940.

It is important to bear in mind that while Buchan did not conceive of himself as an "artist," he was exceptionally well read, took great care over his literary craft, and was consciously in dialogue with those written traditions that he particularly admired. In this last regard, Robert Louis Stevenson was a significant influence on Buchan's views on style (*MHD* 42-3), as were Walter Pater, Gustave Flaubert, Guy de Maupassant, Rudyard Kipling, John Henry Newman, and T. H. Huxley (*MHD* 41, 42). For Buchan, a sound doctrine of writing entailed "the virtue of a clean bare style, of simplicity, of a hard substance and an austere pattern" (*MHD* 35), qualities which he discovered in abundance in the prose of Arthur Balfour (*MHD* 159). Some of the figures Buchan esteemed as masters in the art of fiction included Walter Scott, Alexandre Dumas, père, Victor Hugo, and Honoré de Balzac, among others (*HR* 11), but of these four Scott ranked the very highest: "he left upon me more than the others the impression which the great classical writers leave, of seeing things on a grander scale, of clarifying life, of observing justly and interpreting nobly, of possessing that 'stellar and undiminishable something' which was Emerson's definition of greatness" (*HR* 12). Buchan's attitude towards the aestheticists and modernists who occupied the literary pinnacles during his lifetime was generally disparaging. He looked on them as "porters without luggage" (*HR* 15)—that is, as fixated on form at the expense of content—and noted that he often turned "with comfort from the freakish, stuttering, self-conscious rigmarole of too many modern litterateurs to the clean-cut, efficient prose of a newspaper article" (*HR* 239). As Buchan saw the early twentieth-century literary field, "in our literature to-day prose tends to follow a hundred different models, and since it has no canon and each writer desires to make his style the expression of his temperament, we get a great deal of writing which is careless, fantastic, shapeless, and, to my conservative mind, undeniably bad" (*HR* 238).

These views underpin a literary corpus which has ensured that Buchan has been understood within the still ambiguous category of the "middlebrow" writer. The *OED* defines "middlebrow" in two senses: as a "person who is only moderately intellectual or who has average or limited cultural interests," and as an object "of limited intellectual or cultural value; demanding or involving only a moderate degree of intellectual application, typically as a result of not deviating from convention." Virginia Woolf's view of the middlebrow as a "man, or woman, of middlebred intelligence who ambles and saunters now on this side of the hedge, now on that, in pursuit of no single object, neither art itself nor life itself, but both mixed indistinguishably, and rather nastily, with money, fame, power, or prestige" lurks behind these definitions' depiction of middlebrow writers and artworks as neither this nor that, things parasitic and materialist.[2] But the Buchan now confirmed by academic symposia and scholarship as "middlebrow"—and by general readers throughout the twentieth century as "popular," "thrilling," and "beloved"—cannot be made to conform to these definitions without serious distortions of both his own life and his literary practice. John Baxendale's view of J. B. Priestley as "a serious writer, but a popular one" is, with regard to his would-be place in the literary canon, as good a description of Buchan as one is likely to find, for he combined literary craftsmanship, wit, philosophical acuity, and a committed social conscience with a far-reaching presence in the market that outsold the high modernists against whom he was positioned in complex ways.[3] Buchan was no moderate intellectual: he studied Classics at Brasenose; was widely read in philosophy, history, and the literature of many different national and cultural traditions; and, as his wide range of textual production clearly indicates, was adept at moving between scholarly and creative identities.

That Buchan's fictions themselves are of intellectual and cultural value is the central assumption of this book. It presents Buchan as a writer who wrote in generic forms but who was not unduly constrained by generic conventions. A key postulate of the readings that follow is that if the endings of Buchan's fictions occasionally impart an atmosphere of "neatness" upon the action they describe, that fact should not preclude us from taking seriously the socio-cultural commentaries provided by those fictions before such closures are activated (or, in some cases, after they have occurred). One of the challenges facing sceptical modern readers of

---

[2] Virginia Woolf, *The Death of the Moth and Other Essays*, ed. Leonard Woolf (London: Hogarth Press, 1942), 115.
[3] John Baxendale, *Priestley's England: J. B. Priestley and English Culture* (Manchester: Manchester University Press, 2008), 1.

Buchan is precisely this seeming conflict between a strong socio-cultural conscience and a repeated attraction to the expediently unequivocal ending in which all loose ends are tied up, all ideological difficulties resolved. But, again, this is only half of the story. As we will see, Buchan invokes equivocality and elusiveness in ways that may seem surprising to readers accustomed to the complexities of the so-called "highbrow," to readers who have been encouraged to appreciate difficulty and ambiguity as the sole preserve of modernist writing. Buchan's work has its fair share of simplistic caricatures, but in what follows Buchan is endorsed as a key figure in the evolution of certain kinds of formulaic written modes, but also one capable of challenging them from within. Buchan may be the father of the twentieth-century spy thriller, or he may not, but he is not only that. What should emerge from these pages, it is to be hoped, is a view of a writer committed to *various* forms and styles, to *numerous* ways of thinking.

Take Buchan's literary representations of women, for instance. That Buchan saw women through an equitable lens is borne out in large part by his championing of Woman's Suffrage. That said, it should be pointed out that he had nothing but disdain for Suffragette militancy, which he described as exemplifying "how advocacy should not be conducted" (*CC* 372). In Buchan's literary works women are treated as imaginatively as Buchan's men. His women are frequently powerful figures, either as awesomely potent matriarchs—for example, the "queenly" Margaret Murray in *A Lost Lady of Old Years* (1899), who is described as "a goddess from the void" (*LL* 46) and as an "avenging Amazon" (*LL* 57)—or as unexpectedly formidable ladies who mix prettiness with professionalism, beauty with backbone.[4] Princess Saskia, the ostensibly helpless but in fact accomplished aristocrat in *Huntingtower* (1922), is a stunning girl and a stunningly capable specialist, one whose medical vocation both provides her with skills not possessed by others and renders her incapable of being ostracized through gender rejection: "She was the professional nurse now, absorbed, sexless" (*H* 128). Saskia is in the same line of Buchan women as Mary Lamington, who becomes the wife of Richard Hannay after her first appearance in *Mr Standfast* (1919). On the side of good, Lamington is first encountered as a war nurse but is eventually revealed to be in the employment of the British Government as a secret agent. By the time of her "domestication" through marriage in *The*

---

[4] There are, of course, power*less* women in Buchan's work. For an extended discussion of Buchan's literary representations of women, see Kate Macdonald, "Aphrodite rejected: Archetypal Women in Buchan's Fiction," in Macdonald, *RJB* 153-69.

Three Hostages (1924) she has seemingly turned to the fold of the meek and mild, but her unchallenged comparison of her own character to the Girondin assassin Charlotte Corday (*TH* 192), plus her astounding psychological torture of Dominick Medina, mark her out as something beyond the expectations of the male society by which she is surrounded. As Hannay notes: "Her presence dominated everything, and the very grace of her body and the mild sadness of her eyes seemed to make her the more terrifying. I know now how Joan of Arc must have looked when she led her troops into battle" (*TH* 258). Lamington is seen in this guise only once, but the fact that she is seen in it at all tells us that this "figure of motherhood and pity rather than of awe" (*TH* 259) contains an inimitable force with which to be reckoned.

This is the lesser-known Buchan, who is popularly recognized either for the male heroism of *The Thirty-Nine Steps* (1915) or for Alfred Hitchcock's filmic adaptation of the same work in 1935, *The 39 Steps*. This is in itself a reductive view of the frequency with which Buchan's most famous text has been adapted for the screen. In addition to the Hitchcock movie, *The Thirty-Nine Steps* was filmed in 1959 (dir. Ralph Thomas) and in 1978 (dir. Don Sharp). A remake of Hitchcock's film was planned for 2006 (dir. Robert Towne), but is now due in 2011.[5] The BBC produced an adaptation of Buchan's text in 2008 (dir. James Hawes). The 1978 adaptation, starring Robert Powell, produced a spin-off mini-series called *Hannay*, which ran from 1988-9. Buchan's other work, in turn, has frequently been adapted for the screen and radio. *The Three Hostages* (1924) was adapted for television in 1952, as was *Witch Wood* (1927) in 1954. *Huntingtower* (1922) received similar treatment in 1954. Both *The Three Hostages* and *Huntingtower* were re-adapted for television in 1977 and 1978 respectively. In addition, the following novels have been adapted for radio: *Witch Wood* in 1954 and 1992; *The Three Hostages* in 1960; *The Island of Sheep* (1936) in 1983; *Huntingtower* in 1988; *The Thirty-Nine Steps* in 1989; and *The Courts of the Morning* (1929) in 1993. Alongside all of these treatments, documentaries about Buchan's life and works have appeared at a steady rate.[6]

There is a sense, then, in which *The Thirty-Nine Steps* can be seen as the most inopportune book Buchan ever wrote insofar as it has deflected attention away from some of his more interesting and substantial texts. If it brought him near-universal popular acclaim (an acclaim that extends to our contemporary moment) and sizeable financial reward, then it has

---

[5] http://www.imdb.com/title/tt0393017/ (accessed 8th June 2009).
[6] For more detail about these documentaries, and for further remarks about the above adaptations than I have space for here, see Lownie, *PC* 292-3.

bedevilled his reputation by providing an easy, because frequently misread, target for those unsympathetic towards its narrative craftsmanship and care, and for critics of Buchan's alleged anti-Semitic worldview. In this context, *The Thirty-Nine Steps* has worked as a fulcrum around which broader engagements with the problem of anti-Semitism in Buchan's writing have pivoted.[7] The charge of anti-Semitism typically turns on the objection that Richard Hannay's first-person reportage of the views of one of the novel's key characters, the American agent Franklin P. Scudder, stands in for, or in some way straightforwardly speaks on behalf of, Buchan himself. But by conflating author and narrator in this way, a mix-up that goes unquestioned in some quarters because of Buchan's literary-historical standing, *The Thirty-Nine Steps* is read as anti-Semitic at the expense of what its narrative actually contains. What of the fact that Scudder's anti-Semitism is later contradicted by other characters? What of the fact that this *reported* view *remains* "second-hand" by going unendorsed as a narrative event? By deliberately distorting what Buchan wrote, an injurious fiction is created that still refuses to go away from scholarly circles. Likewise, a tendency of literary historians after the Second World War to focus on his fictional writings, and then only on a small sampling of those, as a central influence upon the twentieth century spy thriller, has contributed to the view of Buchan as little more than a genre fictionist who wrote books about prim and proper gentleman heroes, freezing bathtubs, and crude success-seekers. Outside of Buchan's core audiences, both popular and academic, his writings tend to fall into one of two categories: on the one hand, he is fondly viewed as a well-liked but marginal literary figure; and, on the other, he is seen as a Jew-hating, homophobic, racist dogmatist, one whose fictions advocate his apparent ideological and political conservatisms.

Gertrude Himmelfarb's infamously critical account of Buchan puts these points in representative terms. "There is indeed matter for embarrassment in Buchan's novels," she writes:

> There is the clean, good life which comes with early rising, cold baths, and long immersion in fog and damp, in contrast to the red-eyed, liverish, sluggish, dissolute town dweller. There is the casual bravery, classically understated, of his heroes. [...] There is the blithe provincialism and amateurishness of the spy-adventurer who complains that the natives in a Kurdish bazaar do not understand any 'civilised tongue,' or the member of

---

[7] See, for example, Bryan Cheyette, *Constructions of "the Jew" in English Literature and Society: Racial Representations, 1875-1945*, new edition (Oxford: Oxford University Press, 1995).

Parliament who cannot pronounce 'Boche' names and confuses Poincaré with Mussolini, or the cabinet minister who will not be bothered to read the newspapers while on vacation. There is the penchant for sports that requires every hero (and every respectable villain) to be a first-class shot, and looks upon politics, espionage, and war alike as an opportunity to practice good English sportsmanship. [...] The most serious item in [an] indictment of Buchan is his preoccupation with success, his top-of-the-form ethic.[8]

That said, even Himmelfarb (writing in the 1960s) is prepared to admit that Buchan's fictions are more complex than they might appear. Buchan's heroes and villains may be startlingly success-fixated, yes, but such markings "are the preconditions of their being heroes or villains at all, much as the characters in fairy tales are always the most beautiful, the most exalted, the most wicked of their kind. They are the starting points for romance, not the termination."[9] Buchan's heroes may appear absorbed by action, but they are more than capable of reflection, intellectual debate, and psychological self-torment. Buchan's fictional writing may occasionally seem generically confined, but it is able to switch from sentiment to articulate brilliance, just as Buchan's speeches can switch in a paragraph from questions of national education to those of philosophical nominalism (e.g. *CO* 106).[10]

Buchan's allegedly inflexible Toryism is another fiction imposed upon him by careless reading and grapevine rumour. Edward Leithen's description of "the Tory" in *John Macnab* (1924) as one who believes "that the old buildings were still sound, but they must be swept and garnished, that the ancient weapons were the best, but they must be kept bright and shining and ready for use" closely matches Buchan's own identity as a Tory who "regarded change as a thing undesirable in itself" (*CC* 16), one who argued that "the State is an organism, the slow creation

---

[8] Gertrude Himmelfarb, *The Moral Imagination: From Edmund Burke to Lionel Trilling* (Chicago: Ivan R. Dee, 2006), 135-7.

[9] *Ibid.*, 138.

[10] Buchan can also be fabulously sarcastic, as in the following remarks on stylistic precision: "The other day I read in a reputable newspaper, in a report of Parliamentary proceedings, that the Government 'literally escaped by the skin of their teeth.' I can only say that I wish I had been there to see. My imagination boggles at the picture of the Government beset by a horde of fiery enemies intent upon their bodily destruction, and only separated at one moment by less than the breadth of a hair from death; or another picture of Ministers violently assaulted in the face, and in their escape leaving behind them some indescribably fragile dental covering" (*HR* 246).

of Time; that changes to be organic must be gradual and well considered; that, in short, it is not good to change boats till you have the new one quite ready" (*CC* 17).[11] This Toryism was far from naïvely fixed on rigid continuities. Buchan defended a form of radicalism which left room for self-criticism and change (*MHD* 166), and which was committed to "holding to what was worth holding to in the legacy of the past, but always prepared to jettison lumber" (*MHD* 228). Neither was Buchan uncritical of his own views, taking Toryism to task "when it is used to defend the indefensible privileges of a class, or to oppose all reform." As he put it, if Toryism "is democratic, and looks to the national interests, it will perform a useful public service, and cautious patriots will be attracted to it, just as sanguine and eager patriots will be attracted to Liberalism" (*CC* 17). Class discrimination moved Buchan to passionate rhetoric on a number of occasions, and he refused to fall in line with a traditionalism that upheld class differences derived from outdated feudal infrastructures.[12] As Buchan noted, it "would be a strange anomaly if the class which ultimately controls the decision of the legislature, which is the backbone of our industrial system, and which gives us the personnel of our army and navy, were to be warned off nine-tenths of the soil of the country by an arbitrary minority" (*CC* 45).[13] Buchan defended the rights of the ordinary man, abhorred capitalist exploitation, and articulated accommodating views wherever he felt he could. As we will see more than once in this book, Buchan's politics were insistent but always open to redrafting.

Indeed, it is precisely the act of revision with which Buchan scholarship itself has been busy over the past few decades. Buchan was well regarded during his lifetime as a writer of entertaining, well-constructed fictions, and his popularity has only increased since his death in 1940. However, the Academy has been slow to permit Buchan's entrance into its areas of concern. Thankfully, this situation is now much changed. If he is not yet canonical he is certainly viewed as one of early twentieth-century British culture's most interesting and thought-provoking popular writers.[14] Janet Adam Smith, Buchan's first biographer, showed in

---

[11] Buchan, *John Macnab* (1924) (Edinburgh: Polygon, 2007), 146.

[12] See also *SS2* 95-6.

[13] Writing in 1907 Buchan contended that land "is too often regarded like personal property—something towards which the owner has no obligation save to get the maximum profit out of it for himself. At the same time the country has become thickly peopled, and this land-owning individualism tends to clash with the good of the community" (*CC* 41-2).

[14] To describe Buchan as a "British" writer only draws attention to the fact that he was in fact persistently occupied with the tensions and interrelationships between

John Buchan: A Biography (1965) that his work was worthy of and receptive to scrupulous critical consideration, and David Daniell's excellent *The Interpreter's House: A Critical Assessment of John Buchan* (1975)—which addresses the full range of Buchan's *oeuvre*—proved the point in no uncertain terms. The appearance of the John Buchan Society in 1979, which also inaugurated the *John Buchan Journal*, decisively legitimated this interest. The articles published in the *Journal*'s pages have looked into an enormous range of issues that evince the complexity of Buchan's writings. In 1995 there appeared a second biography, Andrew Lownie's *The Presbyterian Cavalier*, and for the past thirty years or so there has been a steady trickle of Buchan research in a wide range of journals, essay collections, and monographs.[15] 2009 saw published the first essay collection dedicated to Buchan's work: *Reassessing John Buchan: Beyond "The Thirty-Nine Steps"*, edited by Kate Macdonald. This present book aims to complement these studies. As its title suggests, *Modern John Buchan: A Critical Introduction* presents an introductory slice of Buchan's writing and thinking—with a particular emphasis on his engagement with early twentieth-century modernity—as well as offering scholarly interpretations of a representative sampling of his work for those who might already be familiar with his output. It is "critical" in that it tries to toe a line somewhere between a prelude to Buchan's writing and a scholarly investigation of the assumptions informing it. This book is principally concerned with Buchan's fiction, and it offers extended interpretations of Buchan's literary writing in order to underline its identity *as literature*, a status that has largely been denied to it by conservative literary historians.

Buchan did not view himself as a "great" writer, and I will not be making any claims here for him along these lines either, but he was unarguably a *knowledgeable* writer who poured the benefits of wide and reflective reading into the craft of literary production. Both his thrillers and his more introspective fictions are finely produced, combining a profound skill at storytelling with a deep erudition, historical sensibility, and philosophical acumen. Buchan was indubitably one of the twentieth century's finest thriller writers, as well as one of its most interesting, literary critics. Accordingly, I take his fictions as worthy of marked critical attention and as capable of sustaining the same kinds of readings extended

---

his Scottish heritage and English interests. I have not pursued this aspect of Buchan's life and writing in what follows. For an excellent account, see David Goldie, "'Twin Loyalties': John Buchan's England," in Macdonald, *RJB* 29-39.

[15] Kate Macdonald gives a definitive critical history—with which I am entirely in accord—of Buchan scholarship in her *Companion*. See Macdonald, *CMF* 11-14.

to some of his more famous contemporaries. This introduction takes Buchan's fictional work as a route to the political and historical issues he explored in his non-fictional publications. History was particularly significant for Buchan (*CO* 107), and he saw his chief non-literary interests as existing in two main phases: philosophy prior to the Great War, and history in the period thereafter (*CO* 171). With this in mind, I make a number of links between Buchan's literary fictions and his philosophical and historical views, laying especial emphasis on the latter (particularly in Chapter Five, which discusses Buchan's views on history, relativism, and historiography in some detail).

I have not attempted to cover the full range of Buchan's work here. Late works such as *Midwinter* (1923), *The Gap in the Curtain* (1932), and *A Prince of the Captivity* (1933) are mentioned only in passing. Rather than trying to discuss everything I have aimed to familiarize readers with some key aspects of Buchan's literary concerns within the available word count while placing those concerns within the broader context of Buchan's intellectual outlook as a whole. Throughout this book I have tried to discuss texts (such as *The Thirty-Nine Steps* and *Sick Heart River* (1941)) that must be covered in order to give a representative overview of his key literary achievements, as well as consider those texts or literary issues which have not received sustained scholarly or public interest (such as *Huntingtower* and Buchan's relationship with literary modernism). In all cases I have been guided by the relative availability of Buchan's fiction and non-fiction, deciding in some instances to discuss material which is not easily accessible to the general or even the specialist reading public. This has resulted in what some may see as a curious selection of works. For instance, I have said relatively little here about Buchan's short stories and his historical romances, although I have offered a brief account of the artistic and epistemological categories upon which those romances depend. In my view, Buchan is a writer whose commitment to critically engaging with twentieth-century modernity is still underplayed by a significant proportion of his readers and critics. Throughout this book I have tried to show the various ways in which his fictions can be thought of as "modern" as well as part of his broader assessment of the modernity in which he lived. While arguments can be made for the "engaged" properties of Buchan's historical fictions, I opt here for a selection of works explicitly concerned with the modernity of the twentieth century in which Buchan himself played so many key roles.[16]

---

[16] Excellent discussions of Buchan's historical romances can be found in David Daniell's *The Interpreter's House: A Critical Assessment of John Buchan* (1975) and Kate Macdonald's *John Buchan: A Companion to the Mystery Fiction* (2009).

After this opening "Introduction," the remainder of this book is split into five broadly chronological chapters and a final "Conclusion." Chapter Two, "Early Work and Empire," discusses Buchan's youthful novels, as well as his early polemical accounts of empire and imperialism, with reference to *The Half-Hearted* (1900), *A Lodge in the Wilderness* (1906), and *Prester John* (1910). Chapter Three, "Invasions, Spying, Conflict," locates Buchan's most famous works, the Hannay books, in the contexts of the invasion novel tradition and the First World War, and discusses *The Power-House* (1913), *The Thirty-Nine Steps* (1915), *Greenmantle* (1916), and *Mr Standfast* (1919). Chapter Four, "War's Shadow," argues that during the 1920s Buchan makes a sustained effort to come to terms with the effects of the Great War upon modern life, and gives accounts of two texts in which these effects are most keenly felt: *Huntingtower* (1922) and *The Three Hostages* (1924). Chapter Five, "History and Modernism," begins with a run-through of Buchan's views on history and historiography, relates this to the historical romance *Witch Wood* (1927), and then moves on to an extended account of Buchan's critical relationship to literary modernism. Chapter Six, "The Press, Life-Writing, Spirit," discusses *Castle Gay* (1930) with regard to its presentation of newspaper culture, makes links between Buchan's autobiographical *Memory Hold-the-Door* (1940) and literary impressionism, and reflects on the spiritual emphases of Buchan's last great work, *Sick Heart River* (1941). The last chapter, "Conclusion: Secret Agencies," critically teases out some of the ambiguities of Buchan's development of the thriller with close reference to *The Thirty-Nine Steps*, and considers the implied tension between paranoid narrative and paranoid textuality in Buchan's usage of the thriller form.

CHAPTER TWO

EARLY WORK AND EMPIRE

The initial stages of Buchan's literary career were propitious. By 1900, the year of his first "empire" fiction *The Half-Hearted*, he had published three novels: *Sir Quixote of the Moors* (1895), *John Burnet of Barns* (1898), and *A Lost Lady of Old Years* (1899). In 1894 he edited and introduced *Essays and Apothegms of Francis Lord Bacon* for the Walter Scott publishing house, and in 1896 he published his own collection of essays and brief fictional pieces, *Scholar Gipsies*. Buchan did not come down from Brasenose until 1899, but in 1898 he wrote a short history of the college emphasizing its development of good character, its athletic traditions, and its history of scholarly achievement. *Grey Weather*, a collection of short stories, was published in 1899. Buchan edited a fishing anthology, *Musa Piscatrix*, in 1896, and he won the Stanhope essay prize for a piece on Sir Walter Raleigh which was published in 1897. Buchan described his purpose in writing the essay itself as an attempt "to build up from the multitudinous records of the time the vigorous, complex character of the man [...] to sketch his character roughly and crudely, to trace the war of motive which at all times beset him; to find, in short, in his temper and talents some explanation of the cruel circumstances of his fate."[1] Buchan recalled setting up an Ibsen society during his time at Oxford, "which got on well enough until *Ghosts* was read aloud, upon which the members in disgust rejected the name of Ibsen and turned themselves into a dining club called the Crocodiles" (*MHD* 50). His short story "A Captain of Salvation" appeared in the *Yellow Book* in 1896 (alongside stories by George Gissing, Kenneth Grahame, and H. G. Wells), and other stories appeared in the magazine in 1896 and 1897 (Lownie, *PC* 43). In 1898 he became a publisher's reader for John Lane.

    Sir Quixote of the Moors is quite clearly the work of a young man. When it was put forward for reprinting by George Brown in 1918, Buchan replied by saying: "On no account think of bringing out a cheap edition of 'Sir Quixote.' It is a very short book and was written at the age of

---

[1] Buchan, *Sir Walter Raleigh: The Stanhope Essay* (Oxford: Blackwell, 1897), 4, 5.

seventeen. I don't ever want it republished."[2] It is a short book, as Buchan says, but a good, brief read. It concerns the adventures of Jean de Rohaine, the Quixote-esque "Sir" of the book's title, as he journeys through late seventeenth-century Scotland. He meets religious fanatics and a beautiful maiden, and has to grapple with the problems caused by conflicts between self-image and external duty. In addition, *Sir Quixote* establishes one of Buchan's recurrent, self-reflexive themes: the problem of storytelling. Thus Rohaine's confession:

> When I set out to write this history in the English tongue, that none of my own house might read it, I did not know the hard task that lay before me. For if I were writing it in my own language, I could tell the niceties of my feelings in a way which is impossible for me in any other. And, indeed, to make my conduct intelligible, I should forthwith fall to telling each shade of motive and impulse which came to harass my mind. But I am little skilled in this work, so I must needs recount only the landmarks of my life, or I should never reach the end.[3]

This is hardly a "strong" self-reflexive concern with story-telling, but it brings into play that sense of the *constructedness* of narration which recurs throughout Buchan's subsequent novels, such as the moment in *The Thirty-Nine Steps* when Richard Hannay notes that he "seemed to be another person, standing aside and listening to [his] own voice, and judging carefully the reliability of [his] tale" (*TNS* 45). In the end, *Sir Quixote* is a fine example of Buchan's desire "to write fiction in the grand manner, by interpreting and clarifying a large piece of life" (*MHD* 194), a desire he would go on to fulfil in far more successful ways with historical romances such as *Midwinter* (1923), *Witch Wood* (1927), and *The Free Fishers* (1934).

Buchan's time at Oxford followed a trajectory of steadily increasing wealth and literary success: "I must have been at that time an intolerable prig. Consequently the friends I made at first were chiefly hard-working students like myself, or older men in other colleges. Also I was very poor. For two years I could not afford to dine in hall. My Oxford bills for the first year were little over £100, for my second year about £150. After that, what with scholarships, prizes and considerable emoluments from books and articles, I became rather rich for an undergraduate" (*MHD* 48). By the

---

[2] Buchan to George M. Brown, 7th January 1918, B/8/4: *Thomas Nelson Papers*, Edinburgh University Library.
[3] Buchan, *Sir Quixote of the Moors* (1895), ed. Kate Macdonald (Kansas City: Valancourt, 2008), 61.

time Buchan arrived at Oxford he was already considerably well versed in the writings of such philosophical greats as Plato, Kant, and Hegel, and through the work of Arthur Balfour he took on board a pragmatism which made him "judge systems by their historical influence and practical efficiency rather than by their logical perfections" (*MHD* 39). This outlook was soon extended in Oxford to incorporate the influence of Friedrich Nietzsche (*MHD* 49). Oxford prepared Buchan for what might best be described as a "lettered" life of action that combined sweeping material achievement with intellect, scholarship, and philosophical insight. Indeed, in this respect Buchan's life echoed that of one of his earliest fictional creations, John Burnet: "I was born between two stools; for, while I could never be content to stay at home and spend my days among books, on the other hand, the life of unlettered action was repugnant."[4] Most importantly, Buchan's undergraduate years were for him a time in which strong friendships were made with such key individuals as Auberon Herbert, Tommy Nelson, and Raymond Asquith, among others. "Oxford was for me a stabilising influence, but still more was it a mellowing of character through friendship. In my time there was no urgent political or religious question to divide people into militant fraternities. We sought not allies in a cause but friendships for their own sake" (*MHD* 52). Buchan's quasi-Aristotelian extolling of companionship extends throughout his literary work, in which time and again he champions the bond of friendship not only as a primary sort of collectivity but as a virtue in itself, a conduit for the Right and the Good.

The flipsides of these moralities, the Wrong and the Bad, provide the points of departure for Buchan's third novel, *A Lost Lady of Old Years* (1899), which was written when he was just twenty-four years old. The book's first chapter masterfully establishes the Birkenshaw family as a miserly collective whose "penuriousness made their lives frugal and their toils gave them health, so that, a race of strong men, they ran their imperious course, feared in their faults and hated in their virtues" (*LL* 5). This emphasis on "race" is key. As the book's narrator maintains: "It was indeed their pride of race, their inherited spirit, and their greater wealth which alone marked them off from the burly farmers of the countryside. […] Somewhere in the heavy brow and chin of a Birkenshaw there lurked passion and that ferocity which can always awe the born retainer" (*LL* 4). A family of strong physical nature, "[t]here were no weaklings to spoil the family credit, and like a stripped unlovely pine the stock survived, abiding solitary on its hilltop and revelling in storms" (*LL* 4). Precisely how far

---

[4] Buchan, *John Burnet of Barns: A Romance* (London: Bodley Head, 1898), 138.

this pseudo-Darwinian "credit" extends is something of a moot point, for the narrative of *A Lost Lady* opens with a strong emphasis on racial identity underpinned by phrenological characteristics, in which facial features stand in for apparent moral degeneracies. Thus the elder Francis Birkenshaw has "the Birkenshaw high cheekbones, the fleshy chin and the sunken eyes" (*LL* 6); "his father's long limbs and broad back, but in him the former were feeble and knoitering [*sic*], the latter bent in an aimless stoop" (*LL* 6); and an alcohol problem. In the end, "[p]overty and dram-drinking so wrought upon him that soon he was little better than an enfeebled idiot, sitting melancholy on tavern benches and feeding the fire of life on crude spirits" (*LL* 9). Eventually, "a mere wreck of his former wreckage, a parody of a parody" (*LL* 9), the elder Francis dies.

However, there is some light in the gloom, for the elder Francis Birkenshaw does possess "shreds and rags of quality unperceived by his kinsfolk" (*LL* 6), and he acts during a matter of controversial parentage with "an indistinct sense of honour, a certain ill-defined compassionateness of heart, which he scarcely realized and would not have sought to defend" (*LL* 7). His son Francis the younger, with which the novel is centrally concerned, inherits these tensions. A violent child, "as ugly as sin in face, though well-grown and straight in body" (*LL* 11), Francis grows up to be a young man defined by conflicting oppositions. Whereas his two sisters are "honest, fresh-coloured, hearty, and forthcoming to all" (*LL* 12), Francis is "woefully out of place" (*LL* 12) in a home environment in large part defined by charity. At the age of eighteen he retains a violent identity, stabbing (though not killing) a landlord (*LL* 17) and stealing gold from an inebriated gentleman (*LL* 19), thus outgrowing "any vain schemes for a reputable life of citizenship" in "the comedy of life" (*LL* 19). Set in 1745, the year of the second Jacobite Rebellion, *A Lost Lady* charts the adventures of Francis as he struggles with "sudden yearnings towards virtue" (*LL* 28) and betrayals "into compromise, into honesty" (*LL* 35). The novel's true story, in David Daniell's words, is Francis' "own shifting nature, capable of betrayal even when inspired by visionary loyalty, and it finds different shapes in the outside world."[5] Having broken into a house with a fellow ruffian, Francis encounters the disarmingly beautiful Margaret Murray (the wife of Sir John Murray, Secretary to the Young Pretender), who, after mistaking him for a groom, entrusts him with a letter for the rebellious Simon Fraser, the Eleventh Lord Lovat. Francis gets caught up in Prince Charles Edward Stuart's failed pretensions to the

[5] David Daniell, *The Interpreter's House: A Critical Assessment of John Buchan* (London: Nelson, 1975), 67.

British throne, and lives to see Lovat executed and the end of the Jacobite uprising.

A crucial issue here is the relationship between Francis and Margaret Murray, which serves as an index for Birkenshaw's recognition of a "world unknown to him and eternally beyond his reach, mock[ing] him to despair" (*LL* 57). This world arguably is the world of intimacy, a sphere he finds himself placed in contact with by fortune—"Now it chanced that Fate took it upon her to order events for the saving of Francis' soul" (*LL* 15)—but finally one from which Francis remains disconnected, as the end of the novel makes clear: "For a second, he felt an overpowering, jealous craving for this woman, a repugnance to the greyness of his lot. And then it passed, and he could look on her and be thankful for this final spirit" (*LL* 207). Margaret consistently frustrates Birkenshaw's expectations, as in the scene where "[t]he exquisite freshness of her beauty forbade her a place in a gallery of harlots, and to his disgust he found himself forced to regard her with decency" (*LL* 50), and her attractiveness disrupts his comfortable sense of lonely contempt: "At one moment he hated her with deadly vehemence; at the next he would have undergone all humiliation for a sight of her face. The inflated romance which had first driven him out on his travels was centred for the time on this one woman, and with it there followed the bitterness of despair" (*LL* 59). That this world remains beyond Birkenshaw's reach at the conclusion of *A Lost Lady* is a testament to Buchan's ability, already in place by this early stage in his career, to confound the expectations of his readership, and to mix a study of disreputable character with an account of human passions and desires. Indeed, it is more than this, for in denying romantic closure to his acerbic anti-hero Buchan intriguingly calls into question the genre within which the book functions: the broader category of the romance novel itself. As we will see, Buchan returns to this issue more fully in *Huntingtower* in 1922, but it is worth signalling here as evidence of the complexity with which he could weave a tale even within the confines of an uneven and hastily-penned work of youth.

Francis' story plays out against the backdrop of momentous historical events, and so too does the personal narrative of Lewis Haystoun, the protagonist of Buchan's fourth novel, *The Half-Hearted*. Unlike Birkenshaw's story, which, broadly speaking, leads to alienation and death, Haystoun's leads to a death that regenerates himself and saves an empire. Haystoun, initially something of a pathetic figure, travels to India where he foils a Russian invasion of the British Empire's easternmost frontier; in David Trotter's words, Haystoun "dies defending a pass against the entire Russian army, half-hearted no more."[6] Like *A Lost Lady of Old Years*, Buchan's *The Half-Hearted* is an uneven work, quickly written and soon superseded by other fictions, but it is of note for anticipating Kipling's *Kim* (1901) in its choice of setting, its dialogue, and its use of imperial espionage as narrative subject (Macdonald, *CMF* 90). *The Half-Hearted* is also symptomatic of a more general trend in British fiction from this era: that of metropolitan decay. Buchan would argue in "Modern Life and Unrest" (1907) how one could see "a resemblance between the Roman decadence and certain features of modern life as lived in London and New York and other great cities" (*CC* 70-1) at the Edwardian *fin de siècle*, features that for Buchan took the form of municipal over-immigration and rural population decline, extreme differences in class identity, commercialism, hedonism, and forms of vicarious exercise, "which is not so very unlike the old Roman craze for the circus" (*CC* 71).[7] Similarly, *The Half-Hearted* is concerned with a decaying London whose pallid materiality is used to represent a fast-declining, enervated populace. In the heat of summer the capital contrasts sharply with the regenerative airs of the countryside, its paving stones splintered and the window-boxes in Mayfair discoloured and stained, its citizens moving through urban space as tortured, languid souls.[8]

The Half-Hearted enacts the fictional fulfilment of not dwelling "in a churlish and half-hearted manner in the outlying lands," the recommendation Buchan had put forward at the end of the eponymous opening essay to *Scholar Gipsies* (1896).[9] It is a text that marks the beginning of an explicitly "imperial" decade in Buchan's writing that neatly stretches from 1900 to 1910. *The Watcher by the Threshold*, another short story collection, was published by Buchan in 1902. This was followed in 1903 by *The African Colony*, a detailed account of the reconstruction of South Africa following the Boer War that falls somewhere between "a sober political document promoting 'New imperial'

---

[6] David Trotter, "Modernism and Empire: Reading *The Waste Land*," in Colin MacCabe, ed., *Futures for English* (Manchester: Manchester University Press, 1988), 143-53, at 146.

[7] See on this point Lord Appin's reporting of Luke Simeon's attack upon imperialism in *A Lodge in the Wilderness* (1906) as "the 'worship of force.' It represents, [Simeon] says, that tendency of a decadent age which may be observed in the Roman ladies who took their lovers from the prize-ring" (*LW* 59).

[8] Buchan, *The Half-Hearted* (1900) (Teddington: Echo Library, 2006), 26.

[9] Buchan, *Scholar-Gipsies* (London: John Lane, 1896), 24.

consolidation" and "a piece of impressionistic travel writing."[10] It is a long document that imposes upon the African landscape a sense of Scottish identity by means of an "imperial gaze," but it is also a mature assessment of a country's needs during a period of difficult renewal. "South Africa has been in the world's eye for half a century," Buchan writes, "and in the last few years her problems have been so complex that it has been difficult to separate the permanent from the transitory, or to look beyond the mass of local difficulties to the abiding needs of the sub-continent as a whole" (*AC* xi). In 1905 Buchan wrote a legal textbook, *The Law Relating to the Taxation of Foreign Income*, which emerged in part from his experience at the Bar before he joined Milner's so-called South African "Kindergarten" in 1901. His South African years were of decisive importance for Buchan, especially with regard to the practical side of life. "My approach to practical life had been from the side of theory," Buchan remarks of his pre-Africa period: "Now my duties were to be concerned with things for which my education had in no way prepared me, and my daily associates were to be for the most part drawn from worlds of which I had no experience" (*MHD* 96). During his time with Milner Buchan dealt with Boer refugee camps, became head of a special Land Settlement Department, worked as a finance officer, and played a role in establishing plans for the Orange River Colony (Lownie, *PC* 74, 75).

In early 1906 Buchan became an assistant editor for the *Spectator*, and he regularly contributed to its pages on a number of varied topics (Lownie, *PC* 88-9). In February 1907 Buchan took on the editorship of the weekly *Scottish Review*, which he controlled until the paper closed in late 1908. Buchan's articles for the paper fluctuate between domestic and foreign politics, travel writing, socialism and industry, literary criticism, book history, and biography. There is even an article on "Flying Machines and Motor Cars" (1908), in which Buchan takes to task Wells' *When the Sleeper Awakes* for its "gruesome picture" of a human race "driven to revive the habits of their first progenitors, and spend most of [its] life underground" (*CC* 378).[11] Buchan's literary criticism for the *Scottish Review* includes discussions of Shakespeare and Raleigh, the novel, George Meredith, the making of books, journalistic hysteria, the philosophy of reprinting, the Scots tongue, and a comparison between "old" and "new" journalistic techniques. Articles such as "The Making of Books" (1907) and "The Philosophy of the Reprint" (1907) reveal Buchan

---

[10] Jeremy Foster, "John Buchan's 'Hesperides': Landscape Rhetoric and the Aesthetics of Bodily Experience on the South African Highveld, 1901-1903," *Ecumene* 5: 3 (July 1998), 323-47, at 325.

[11] For an intriguing reference to Wells' *The Time Machine* see *SS3* 66.

to be firmly in tune with the effects of modernity upon literary and non-literary production, while "The Old Journalism and the New" (1908) discusses the influence of tabloid journalism upon public opinion, an area of debate to which he returned in *Castle Gay* (1930).

A number of Buchan's articles for the *Spectator* were published in book form as *Some Eighteenth Century Byways* (1908), which also reprinted Buchan's writing from Blackwood's *Maga*, the *Atlantic Monthly*, and the *Quarterly Review*. It is an important text, which includes a key discussion of John Bunyan, one of Buchan's life-long influences, and his early rejection of Tolstoy's philosophy of pacifism, which he criticized in his "London Letters"—a section of the *Scottish Review*—for what he saw as its ruinous oversimplifications of human identity and experience: "[Tolstoy] preaches a quietism which shows so false a conception of human nature that it is difficult to realize that this crude preacher is the shrewd critic of life who wrote the novels. He suffers not from too much, but from too little, idealism, for he cannot see beyond the horrors of war and the occasional follies of nationalism to the great fact of patriotism" (*CC* 387). In "Count Tolstoi and the Idealism of War" Buchan objected to Tolstoy on several grounds: he found fault with the naïvely optimistic streak he felt Tolstoy's position implied, arguing that it had little purchase on contemporary realities; he opposed the view that the problem of war could be eliminated by appealing to a universal spiritual morality; he accused Tolstoy of an apathy the consequences of which remained uncertain and potentially ruinous; and he insisted that Tolstoy's denunciation of war rested at bottom upon a materialism solely contrived to mitigate psychological and physical torment.[12]

Buchan answered Tolstoy's idealism by suggesting that conflict contains an ennobling quality of its own, and he claimed that the most appropriate sense in which to conceptualize warfare is not through the language of atrocity but "to emphasise the spiritual and idealist element which it contains" (*SEB* 298). Buchan suggested elsewhere that despite "all its cruelty and futility [war] has a power of raising men to their highest and exhibiting human nature at its greatest" (*HR* 178). To Buchan's way of thinking, for all its tragic loss of life and catastrophic upheavals, war accentuates the dignity of the human condition by drawing attention to mankind's capacity for self-sacrifice on behalf of values beyond the realm

---

[12] In *The Island of Sheep* (1919)—the book written by Buchan and his wife under the double pseudonym 'Cadmus and Harmonia'—Buchan would write: "'A great idealist often finds it hard to understand other idealisms than his own, and ends by being rather specially *terre-à-terre*'" (Cadmus and Harmonia, *The Island of Sheep* (London: Hodder and Stoughton, 1919), 103).

of material desires. He argued that "to prohibit men to fight for a cause in which they believe—that is, to devote to it their most valuable possessions, their lives—is to strike at the root of faith" and to deny the worth of this fight "between the real and the ideal" is "to cast doubt upon the highest instinct of our mortal nature" (*SEB* 297). Buchan maintained that a pacifism such as Tolstoy's aimed for peace at the cost of variation across cultures and between moral selves, and he refused to assent to an outlook which silenced difference in the name of appeasement (*SEB* 299- 300). This indicates that Buchan was neither indifferent to the precariousness of a world populated by a multiplicity of ideologies and passions nor uninterested in efforts, such as Norman Angell's *The Great Illusion* (1910), to prevent the world from drifting into global hostilities. At the same time, it underscores the centrality of pluralism within Buchan's worldview, an attitude of mind resolute in the belief that a monochrome humanity stood for nothing less than a victorious decadence.[13]

Moreover, *Some Eighteenth Century Byways* is of especial interest for Buchan's early account of history and historical writing, an account he would go on to extend in key ways in later works. In part this boiled down to questions of style. Buchan contended that, in addition to refraining from "insisting upon obvious morals," the "historian must guard himself carefully from effective exaggeration, though the times seem to adapt themselves to it, he must be scrupulous in his use of authorities, and chary of accepting traditional views of character and policy" (*SEB* 104). Buchan favoured the use of simple language in historical writing as much as he praised the employment of straightforward expression in philosophy, and in a discussion of Arthur Balfour he wrote that "far greater is the originality of a man who deals with common matters in simple language, and yet forces the reader to a new point of view" (*SEB* 276). What is most noticeable here, though, is Buchan's insistence upon the "interestedness" of the historian's calling. Dismissing the claims of an "objective" impersonalism, Buchan argued that "[p]artisan history, provided the historian be honest with his authorities, is to our mind the more trustworthy form, for if the reader be aware of a bias he can allow for it, and is not misled by partiality cloaked under an air of judicial detachment" (*SEB* 115). Such a view anticipates Buchan's critique of "scientific" or "total" historical objectivism in later essays such as "The Causal and the Casual in History" (1929) and "The Most Difficult Form of Fiction"

---

[13] Michael Redley, "John Buchan and *The Great Illusion*," *John Buchan Journal* 37 (Autumn 2007), 30-5.

(1929), which I discuss later. Buchan's view was that historical writing should reflect the interests and mannerisms of its author, since, as he put it, it is "hard for a man to write without prejudice on the many matters he treats of, for the history comes down to within living memory, and some of these old questions divide men in our own day" (*SEB* 169).

The key dividing issue for Buchan during this period was empire. If the question of empire united a Britain at the peak of its powers, it also divided many of its adherents over the issue of what, precisely, empire signified in the post-Boer War epoch. This was no hitherto unencountered problem. As Ebenezer Wakefield notes in *A Lodge in the Wilderness* (1906): "'I need hardly [say] that a common ideal, held with a difference, has proved in the past the most potent of disruptive forces'" (*LW* 34). This text, arguably the most important book Buchan wrote during the Edwardian period, appeared one year after Wells' *A Modern Utopia* (1905) and is comparably nuanced in its account of an ideal form of collective life, even if it locates that life within the contours of an imperialism that Wells had for many years been busily subjecting to disdainful critique. In A. E. MacRobert's words, *A Lodge in the Wilderness* "cannot be evaluated as a novel nor as the prototype of a series of political treatises. Its importance is essentially that of a source-book for views on Imperialism in 1906."[14] Sitting somewhere between fictionality and reportage, *A Lodge* borrows from W. H. Mallock's *The New Republic* (1878), a satire on the Oxford intelligentsia of that book's time, by presenting an account of empire in the form of a symposium held in Musuru, a house in East Africa owned by Francis Carey (who has generally been read as a thinly-fictionalized Cecil Rhodes). The book's "plot" takes the form of a series of discussions between prominent society members who go to Musuru, "a place to work, to talk, to think, but not to idle in" (*LW* 19), in order "to make a short sojourn in the wilderness" (*LW* 14) so as to theorize anew the imperial creed during a period of deep unease.[15] A central argument of the book is that the imperial project "'is not a creed or a principle, but an attitude of mind'" (*LW* 58). It is a stock-taking work which provides, in Carey's words, "the occasion to examine ourselves and find the reason of that faith which is in us" (*LW* 27). If the book comes to no fixed conclusion about the nature of imperialism it

---

[14] A. E. MacRobert, "*A Lodge in the Wilderness* (1906): A Reappraisal," *John Buchan Journal* 19 (Autumn 1998), 27-32, at 29.

[15] Thus Buchan in *The African Colony*: "Ideals are all very well in their way, but they are apt to become very dim lamps unless often replenished from the world of facts and trimmed and adjusted by wholesome criticism" (*AC* x-xi).

nonetheless emphasizes the importance of discourse and debate, even if discussion takes place here only between the privileged few.

The book's complexity owes much to its form. Each word of its title is precisely chosen: *A Lodge in the Wilderness*. The opening indefinite article presents the book's statements as but possible contentions among others (a move backed up by its use of the dialogue-symposium format), and the choice of "Lodge," as opposed to the more Conradian "Outpost," represents imperialism as a temporary mode of dwelling in the world that is but a stage in a longer journey. In this way, imperialism is presented as an ongoing, exacting project. "Sound government," Buchan wrote in *The African Colony* (1903), "is not as revolutionary doctrinaires used to think, the outcome of the grace of God and a flawless code of abstractions. It means a perpetual effort, a keen sense of reality, a constant facing and adjusting of problems. And it is one of the laws of life that this high faculty is inconsistent with extreme luxury and ease" (*AC* 31). The final word in the book's title, "Wilderness," is no less important. With its echoes of the natural world and of a more abstract sense of chaotic flux, the lodge in this wilderness is thus both a point of civilization within a broader rough country and a retreat from modernity's shapelessness, a state of unrest that it is the imperialist's mission to bring under control.[16] That these notions may now appear out of touch with the wants and needs of those living in the very spaces targeted for imperial rule is not the issue here. Buchan was hardly alone in his views of empire as a force for good during this period, and he considered that the days of his experiences in Africa "were the days when a vision of what the Empire might be made dawned upon certain minds with almost the force of a revelation" (*MHD* 124). For Buchan, as for many others, imperialism was a mechanism of religious power, an extension of God's will.[17]

Alan Sandison writes that "[i]nvesting empire with an altogether ecclesiastical significance [Buchan] looked on it as a God-given means whereby man in his secular condition could be integrated with his spiritual ideal."[18] This is borne out by the views put forward in *A Lodge in the*

---

[16] In 1935 Buchan wrote of Canada: "To-day she is still the pioneer, but a pioneer in the overthrowing of a more dangerous barbarism, in driving a path through a more tangled wilderness, the wilderness of human fears and human perversities" (*CO* 14).

[17] It is this very attitude that Conrad so scornfully satirizes in *Heart of Darkness* (1899).

[18] Alan Sandison, *The Wheel of Empire: A Study of the Imperial Idea in Some Late Nineteenth and Early Twentieth-Century Fiction* (New York: St Martin's Press, 1967), 149.

Wilderness. Buchan noted in the Preface to the book's 1916 reprint that the British Empire "is a mystic whole which no enemy may part asunder, and our wisest minds are now given to the task of devising a mechanism of union adequate to this spiritual unity" (*LW* x). And yet it is in the opinions of the figures of the narrative proper that this religious emphasis comes out most clearly. For Lady Lucy Gardner, imperialism withstands concise definition precisely insofar as it is "'not a creed but a faith'" (*LW* 27); as she argues: "'You cannot carve an epic on a nutshell or expound Christianity in an aphorism. If I could define Imperialism satisfactorily in a sentence I should be very suspicious of its truth'" (*LW* 27-8). Or take Eric Lowenstein, who defines it as "'the spirit which giveth life as against the letter which killeth. It means a renunciation of old forms and conventions, and the clear-eyed facing of a new world in the knowledge that when the half-gods go the true gods must come'" (*LW* 29). Supporting the book's spiritualist emphases is a holistic account of imperialism as an organic construct. Wakefield describes this as "'the closer organic connection under one Crown of a number of autonomous nations of the same blood, [...] a racial aristocracy considered in their relation to the subject peoples, a democracy in their relation to each other'" (*LW* 28).[19] In this respect *A Lodge in the Wilderness* dovetails with Buchan's own bilateralist and organicist conception of empire, which he articulated elsewhere as "the foundation of a common Imperial policy—an Empire of States, which, while free to follow their national interests, are yet parts of a greater organism and rest upon a wider ideal" (*CC* 90).[20]

A Lodge in the Wilderness clearly depicts empire as a form of utopianism: "It was his business, [Carey] said, to show the world a more excellent way" (*LW* 12).[21] Looking back on this period in *Memory Hold-the-Door*, Buchan wrote: "My political experience at the time was nil, and my views were shallow and ill-informed—inclinations rather than principles. I believed profoundly in the possibilities of the Empire as a

---

[19] Thus Buchan: "[T]he Empire is an alliance into which all the members enter on equal terms. But it is more than a mere alliance – it is a family partnership and a working partnership. There is the bond of blood and a common ideal between the members, and, since they work for a common purpose, there must be some machinery for joint deliberation and joint action" (*CC* 87).

[20] For a further sampling of Buchan's comments on imperialism and organicism, see *CC* 4, 17, 25-6, 68, and 90. See also *SHR* 35. For Buchan and bilateralism see *CC* 93-4.

[21] Compare this with Buchan's later view of Caesar, whose dream was of "a new kind of empire, the strength of which would lie not in its wealth and its relics of an older civilisation but in the quality of its people" (*MD* 63).

guardian of world peace, and as a factor in the solution of all our domestic problems" (*MHD* 144). Buchan's qualified endorsement of his attitude to empire at this time is reflected in *A Lodge in the Wilderness* through Carey, who looks to imperialism as a liberal "creed beyond parties, a consuming and passionate interest in the destiny of his people" (*LW* 13). That said, although Buchan follows the views of Carey in some respects, he is careful not to make Carey his spokesperson, as the latter's voice, like the text's own relativism, is presented as but one voice among numerous alternatives. This is of especial significance with regard to Carey's objectivist leanings, which are represented here as in tension with less "top-down" accounts of social change.[22] In Carey's view "'the great thing in the world is to reach the proper vantage-ground,'" as for him this leads to a form of objective knowledge that "'can only be known to the man on the hill-top'" (*LW* 31-2). Adopting a kind of blueprint rationalism, in which the goals of empire are determined in advance of empire's application to real life contexts, Carey recommends that "'[i]f we cannot create a new heaven, we can create a new earth'" (*LW* 32). Here, the non-representative status of Carey's views is strongly implied by the fact that at one of his most rhetorically-charged moments the attention of his audience lies elsewhere (*LW* 32).[23]

Buchan goes to some lengths to suggest that Carey's "blueprint" politics are still accommodating of difference, a point made through the latter's claim that empire can be phrased "'in a thousand ways without exhausting its content'" (*LW* 28). As Buchan put it elsewhere, "[t]here is hardly a political question which is capable of a simple answer, scarcely an evil which admits of a single cure" (*CC* 46). Whether or not *A Lodge in the Wilderness* succeeds in this effort is something of a moot point, but I would argue that the book attempts to preserve a tolerant spirit of acceptance, as I have already claimed, through its use of the dialogue form. Plato's writings are referred to at an early point in the book (*LW* 35), and it is precisely in imitation of Platonic debate that Buchan makes his

---

[22] There seemingly is a link here to the views of Mr Vennard in "A Lucid Interval" (1910): "'Human destinies cannot be treated as if they were inert objects under the microscope. The cold-blooded logical way of treating a problem is in almost every case the wrong way'" (*SS2* 127).

[23] Looking back on his early imperial period, Buchan self-critically observed: "We were inclined to grandiloquence and rhetoric in our perorations at imperial banquets. We were prone to boast of having an Empire on which the sun never set—but, as Mr. Chesterton once said, there is not much charm in an Empire which has no sunsets! In a word, we were in peril of worshipping quantity and size and mass" (*CO* 188).

characters articulate and take to task the idea of empire at a key moment in its development.[24] Like a play, *A Lodge* is presented with a character list at the beginning, thus suggesting that it might be read as a kind of Socratic debate. But even if the book does not escape from the confines of third-person narration into a fully-fledged Platonic dialogue, it is surely significant that the third person narratorial voice is not *suppressed* in this text but, rather, relegated as subordinate to the opinions raised in the book's dialogues. In this way, Buchan tries to keep "empire" destabilized, thus making it out to be an ideological machinery always open for redefinition. And there is even a hint of Wells' notion of the "kinetic utopia" in *A Lodge*'s view of "change" as being at the heart of a successfully modern imperialism. In *A Modern Utopia* Wells' narrator claims that "the Modern Utopia must be not static but kinetic, must shape not as a permanent state but as a hopeful stage leading to a long ascent of stages."[25] Buchan was critical of Wellsian utopianism (*CC* 72), but there does seem to be a prefiguring in Buchan's work of this view through *A Lodge*'s account of self-editing and redaction as the essence of an imperial framework (*LW* 71-2).[26]

I have stressed the provisionality of *A Lodge in the Wilderness* because, as critics before me have argued, the book's high level of generality (that is, its abstract treatment of the question of empire) does not work entirely in its favour. For Kate Macdonald, the text's "exclusivity is signalled by all-embracing terms such as 'the people' and 'we,' when it is quite clear that 'we' are from a very limited social circle indeed. Basic economics are ignored, making the value of the theoretical discussion equally limited" (Macdonald, *CMF* 113).[27] The paramount "imaginative" engagement with the question of empire that Buchan wrote during this

---

[24] This is not to imply that *A Lodge* imagines British imperial authority as parallel to the authority of the Platonic city-state. Note that in *The King's Grace* Buchan writes: "In the Platonic utopia the king was the philosopher; it is more important that he should be the plain man" (*KG* 159). See also *CO* 77-8.

[25] H. G. Wells, *A Modern Utopia* (1905), ed. Francis Wheen (London: Penguin, 2005), 11.

[26] Buchan held to this point throughout his life. He later wrote of imperial democracy that "we must constantly overhaul our stock of political ideas and reject what is ossified and out of date, for it is only by such recensions that the enduring truths are seen in their true perspective" (*CO* 124-5).

[27] Juanita Kruse notes that it was in *A Lodge in the Wilderness* where Buchan's faith in Milner's idealism "ran away with him, and he made of imperialism a faith, almost a religion, though with a few cautious checks on his own exuberance" (*John Buchan (1875-1940) and the Idea of Empire* (Lewiston: Edwin Mellen Press, 1989), 75).

period remains *Prester John* (1910). Written in the year which, according to Virginia Woolf, human character changed, *Prester John* is concerned with the changes in character of two human individuals in particular: David Crawfurd, a young Scotsman who goes to South Africa in search of riches and to make something of his life, and John Laputa, a parish priest who is revealed as a native Christian minister calling for African revolt against Western imperialism. Laputa's nationalist slogan is "Africa for the Africans," it is explained to Crawfurd, the former's chief point being "'that the natives had had a great empire in the past, and might have a great empire again'" (*PJ* 73). Laputa is thus a representative of Ethiopianism, one of the first, late-nineteenth century gestures towards colonial freedom in this region that sought an Africanized Christianity through which tribalism and ethnic identity could be re-asserted despite colonial subjugation. Buchan observed in *The African Colony* that South Africa "is an old country, as old as time, the prey of many conquerors, but with it all a patient and mysterious land. Civilisations come and go, and after a millennium or two come others who speculate wildly on the relics of the old" (*AC* 17).[28] Likewise *Prester John*, with its images of conflicting ideas of the Good Life, is centrally concerned with questions of ownership, land, and ancestry, all of which reaches its climax in the conflict between the competing imperial projects of Laputa's uprising and Crawfurd's Britishness, troped here as a dissonance between the latter's modernity and, by means of the former, the return of the Christian greybeard Prester John.

Laputa is immediately characterized by Crawfurd as "beyond the beat of our experience" (*PJ* 11); that is, as beyond the familiar epistemological categories held by Crawfurd and his teenaged friends during their first encounter with the black minister. But to some extent Laputa and the primitivism he signifies remains beyond the beat of "Western" experience throughout the novel as a whole. One sign of this alterity is the way in which native dexterity is constructed by Crawfurd and his allies as a form of supernatural trickery, as in their references to Laputa as a "wizard" (*PJ* 42, 55), and their distrust of "the wonders of Kaffir telegraphy" (*PJ* 132). By this means, it is reported, Laputa and his followers "'can send news over a thousand miles'" (*PJ* 54) as speedily as its mechanized, Western equivalent, the telephone. However, it is surely significant that this skill is never mentioned by the novel's South African native characters: it is more

---

[28] One way in which Buchan incorporates the notion of South Africa as steeped in antiquity is through the character of the old blind man in the Rooirand Cave, whose face is described by Crawfurd as "seamed and lined and shrunken, so that he seemed as old as Time itself" (*PJ* 48).

accurate to speak of it as a "skill" imposed upon them by Crawfurd and Arcoll so as to rationalize an otherwise inexplicable ability to confound Laputa's enemies. Here the novel explicitly focuses on the issue of perception, an issue signalled in symbolic terms through Crawfurd's use of "Zeiss glass" (*PJ* 44) binoculars. With this appliance Crawfurd is able to survey the African veldt with scientific precision, but such an ability stands in stark contrast to Crawfurd's *inability* to perceive native forms of subjectivity except through the vocabularies of ethnic ascendancy that have produced his psyche.[29] Thus *Prester John* returns in part to Conrad— a link implicitly signalled in Buchan's text via Crawfurd's reference to having "looked into the heart of darkness" (*PJ* 110)—and his negative assessment (via delayed decoding) of the processes of imperial vision.[30]

Prester John engages with several issues, among them the illegal diamond trade and the history of Portuguese colonialism in South Africa.[31] However, for my purposes what is especially significant about the book is its relativization of the idea of empire, its meticulous analysis of the common ground between "authorized" and "intolerable" creeds of racial dominance, ethical purity, and religious zealotry. It is noted in Crawfurd's first-person narration that, during his first encounter with Laputa on the Kirkcaple shore in Scotland, "[t]here was something desperately uncanny about this great negro, who had shed his clerical garments, and was now practising some strange magic alone by the sea" (*PJ* 13). Despite Laputa's naked difference (in both senses of the phrase), Crawfurd cannot help but see some kind of reciprocal quality that ties Laputa up with the Britishness to which he is opposed. As Freudian psychoanalysis might phrase it, Laputa's uncanniness—that "something" described in "The Green Glen"

---

[29] Arcoll is as bad as Crawfurd in this respect: "I asked about Laputa's knowledge of our preparations. Arcoll was inclined to think that he suspected little. The police and the commandos had been kept very secret, and, besides, they were moving on the high veld and out of the ken of the tribes. Natives, he told me, were not good scouts so far as white man's work was concerned, for they did not understand the meaning of what we did" (*PJ* 80-1).

[30] I am thinking here of those moments in Conrad's work, and in *Heart of Darkness* especially, which "put the reader in the position of being an immediate witness of each step in the process whereby the semantic gap between the sensations aroused in the individual by an object or event, and their actual cause or meaning, [is] slowly closed in his consciousness" (Ian Watt, *Conrad in the Nineteenth Century* (Berkeley, CA: University of California Press, 1981), 270).

[31] For a discussion of *Prester John*'s representation of the Portuguese see Maria Teresa Pinto Coelho, "The Image of the Portuguese in the British Novel of Empire: *King Solomon's Mines* and *Prester John*," in Theo D'haen and Patricia Krüs, eds, *Colonizer and Colonized* (Amsterdam: Rodopi, 2000), 357-69.

(1912) as "not terrible exactly, or threatening, but inhumanly strange" (*SS2* 199)—is both the sign of an "exotic" subjectivity and a mysterious, eerie closeness. References to Laputa as Crawfurd's "enemy" (e.g. *PJ* 15, 17, 77, 83) abound in this text, and it is in this way that *Prester John* intensifies the idea of Laputa as not just an "other" but, rather, an other (as all others must be) in relation to something else, a something to which Laputa is bound in military and political struggle, as well as a fight for individual identity. In this regard it is telling that Laputa is recalled by Crawfurd in the following terms: "I remember looking back and seeing the solemn, frowning faces of the cliffs, and feeling somehow shut in with this unknown being in a strange union" (*PJ* 11). Laputa emerges as a figure largely defined by and through the imperial ideologies he resists; he is the converse, "unhomely" shadow of expansionist projects no less uncompromising than his own.[32]

One way of reading Laputa's uprising is as an unwelcome repeat of the Indian Mutiny against British rule during the late 1850s. This possibility is raised by means of the character of Mr Wardlaw, a schoolmaster, who notes that a successful African native imperialism, one of "powerful military discipline," would lead to a "'second and bloodier Indian mutiny'" (*PJ* 53). Buchan wrote that the ongoing instabilities of the Indian subcontinent were still problematic issues during the Edwardian period. He maintained that while the Indian Mutiny had been "mainly religious" (*CC* 105) in nature, turn-of-the-century Indian discontent was primarily a *political* phenomenon, thus making it, in Buchan's eyes, "by far our foremost Imperial problem" (*CC* 109). Such a problem took the form of a disenfranchised people demanding sovereignty during a time and in a place where such independence was not only impossible to bestow but also unwise, as Buchan saw it, to adopt. For him, the "middle road" of co-operation, whereby it is the duty of the imperialist "to assist and cultivate every legitimate Indian aspiration, and to train the native slowly to take part in the work of government" (*CC* 109), was the right course, and he rejected desires such as "an autonomous and united India" as "wild non-historical dreams" (*CC* 111). But events like the Indian Mutiny derive from the split between what a ruler considers right and proper and what is considered to be so by the ruled (in the very idea of what "reasonably" counts as a "legitimate aspiration," in other words). In *Prester John*'s account of Laputa's insurrectionary aspirations some difficult notions (notions as difficult as the "political" nature of Edwardian Indian

---

[32] The figure of Prester John is conceived in "The Kings of Orion" (1906) as "'a conqueror,'" the head of "'a race of warriors, but first and foremost ... a statesman'" (*SS2* 81).

unhappiness) are brought to bear on Crawfurd's adolescent view of the socio-political world. Crawfurd is very much an imperial subject, one as much formed by the civilizing rhetorics of the British Empire as Laputa stands against them.[33] That Crawfurd narrates the story is key in this respect. It is by means of his first-person viewpoint that Buchan invites his audience to see *Prester John* as both a satiric take on an immature understanding of the complexities of imperial politics *and* as a chance to "step into" that role to enable contemporary defenders of empire to reflect on their own belief systems.[34]

In this way *Prester John* does not break from Buchan's faith in the beneficial possibilities of empire. Instead, it subjects them to critical inspection. Crawfurd's journey from youthful "Empire boy," in Joseph Bristow's terminology, to self-made young man is no less a journey for the discourses through which his subjectivity has been formed.[35] Of central importance to this journey is the astonishing moment when Crawfurd feels afresh the mesmeric seductiveness of imperial rhetoric, a rhetoric now deployed by Laputa as opposed to his imperial "masters." Invoking a future in which "[a]nother Ethiopian empire would arise, so majestic that the white man everywhere would dread its name, so righteous that all men under it would live in ease and peace" (*PJ* 105), Laputa becomes for Crawfurd "more king than priest, more barbarian than Christian. It was as a king that he now spoke" (*PJ* 105). And yet it is a Christian doctrine that Laputa espouses. "I knew his heart," Crawfurd notes, "black with all the lusts of paganism. I knew that his purposes was to deluge the land with blood. But I knew also that in his eyes his mission was divine, and that he felt behind him all the armies of Heaven" (*PJ* 104). That Crawfurd is tempted by Laputa's language is a significant gesture on Buchan's part,

---

[33] The "inverse" moment when Crawfurd attempts to fool Laputa into thinking he is critical of Empire, when in fact Crawfurd is really only pretending to be so to lure the latter into a false sense of security, gives away his political affinities: "I told him affectionately that I liked natives," Crawfurd notes, "that they were fine fellows and better men than the dirty whites round about. I explained that I was fresh from England, and believed in equal rights for all men, white or coloured. God forgive me, but I think I said I hoped to see the day when Africa would belong once more to its rightful masters" (*PJ* 84).

[34] It is of interest here that Buchan saw Canada as having answered the difficulties of South Africa in this respect: "Canada has solved the problem which South Africa has to face. She has achieved union without sacrificing local patriotism. She has welded two strong and very different races into one nation" (*CC* 99). See also *CO* 11-12.

[35] Joseph Bristow, *Empire Boys: Adventures in a Man's World* (London: Harper Collins Academic, 1991).

since with this move Buchan strongly hints at the contingency of Crawfurd's imperial identity: if so strong an imperial subject can be swayed (albeit momentarily) by an alternative, "primitive" vision of a theocratic imperialism, then the British imperial project itself may have less secure foundations than its ideologues would have others accept. Crawfurd's ultimate resistance to Laputa's Ethiopianism is the point at which *Prester John*'s faith in the contingent, but authentic and accountable, nature of the British imperial project is restored. To quote Lee Horsley: "What has been preserved in the successful resistance to Laputa, then, is precisely this sense of responsibility, the special 'gift' of the white race, and what, in essence, is thought to separate British political rule from the dark, dynamic attractions of a complete regression to charismatic domination."[36]

Laputa's attractiveness is one of many dividing lines in *Prester John*. Freud suggests that uncanniness entails the parallel mechanisms of "being attracted to" and "being repulsed by," and it is by dint of the paradoxes caused by this tension that *Prester John* activates a range of homosocial intonations.[37] Consider the following description:

> [Laputa] thanked me with a grave dignity which I had never seen in any Kaffir. As my eye fell on his splendid proportions I forgot all else in my admiration of the man. In his minister's clothes he had looked only a heavily built native, but now in his savage dress I saw how noble a figure he made. He must have been at least six feet and a half, but his chest was so deep and his shoulders so massive that one did not remark his height. He put a hand on my saddle, and I remember noting how slim and fine it was, more like a high-bred woman's than a man's. Curiously enough he filled me with a certain confidence. (*PJ* 83-4)

Caution must be taken when interpreting a passage such as this. Apparently loaded terms such as "his splendid proportions" and "he filled me" can be forced into misleading accounts of homoeroticism at the expense of historical specificity. It is necessary to bear in mind that what some can now take as homoerotic may once have been homosocial without being sexually evocative. Postmodernity's "playfulness" can sometimes obscure the fact that "queer" (a word which recurs throughout

---

[36] Lee Horsley, *Fictions of Power in English Literature, 1900-1950* (London: Longman, 1995), 77.

[37] For an extended, if problematic, account of *Prester John*'s homosocial and homoerotic investigations see Craig Smith, "Every Man Must Kill the Thing He Loves: Empire, Homoerotics, and Nationalism in John Buchan's *Prester John*," *Novel* 28: 2 (Winter 1995), 173-202.

Prester John) did not mean "homosexual" in 1910.[38] In the present context
it should be noted that *Prester John* allows such a seemingly eroticized
account of the male body as the one quoted above to be read not as
homosexual desire but as youthful admiration. Not forgetting that these
words are meant to be *Crawfurd's*, rather than *Buchan's*, this passage can
also be seen as an attempt to decode racial difference in the familiar
(familiar, that is, to Crawfurd) terms of nobility and fine breeding. If it
must be read as desire then at least two kinds of such "want" present
themselves: on the one hand it might be the inexperienced desire of a
young man unable to express his esteem of a more powerful man in
anything but the de-focussed idiom of longing, a "crush" on a more
powerful, aristocratic elder; and on the other hand it could well be some
form of inter-racial attraction, a colonial fascination with a man seen as a
primitive, noble savage.

    All that said, Crawfurd's attraction to Laputa is signalled throughout
Prester John with sufficient frequency to warrant finding in it some kind
of psychodynamic, be it sexual or otherwise, and it is this dynamic that
Prester John's closures work hard to suppress. There is, I am suggesting, a
gap between the level of the author (Buchan) and the level of character at
work here. This disjunction enables us to read the actions of particular
characters within the story as in conflict with the way in which those same
actions are described by the characters performing them. Crawfurd may
deferentially observe Laputa's death as a "half-remorseful spectator of a
fall like the fall of Lucifer" (*PJ* 179), but in one sense Laputa is "killed
off" from the moment of his first appearance through the associations in
his surname. Although *Prester John* takes a complex view of this
Ethiopianist revolutionary, the air of impractical utopian politics attributed
to him by the Swiftian "Laputa"—the airborne island in *Gulliver's Travels*
inhabited by prophets whose social idealisms are completely unworkable
in practice—renders his vision of African hegemony implicitly false, a
"utopian" project somewhat in the Marxist sense of being unrealistic in
contrast to a more scientific view of the methods by which community is
achieved. *Prester John*, in other words, weighs the utopianism of *A Lodge
in the Wilderness* against the utopianism of Laputa, finding in the latter an
intolerable idealism that must be contained. Crawfurd's reference to
having been "living in a dream-world" (*PJ* 106) while under the spell of
Laputa's "perverted" Christian rhetoric indicates both a mesmeric effect
and perhaps alludes to what Buchan and many others would have seen as
the impracticable nature of Laputa's politics. This split, between the views

[38] The *OED* dates the earliest use of "queer" as meaning "homosexual" to 1914.

of characters and the workings of form, recurs throughout Buchan's fictions. It appears most notably in *Mr Standfast*'s treatment of pacifism, which is endorsed through the character of Launcelot Wake but problematized by the symbolic forms that characterize him in the first place.[39] It is an encoded form of what Buchan himself called England's "national gift of meiosis" (*MHD* 168), the "power of domesticating the strange and the terrible and making portents homely" (*MHD* 168-9).[40] Laputa must be silenced precisely because, in addition to his primitive otherness, he represents the force of the threat within, a portent *of* the home *as well as* one from beyond its borders. Buchan returns to this issue again and again throughout his writing, and *Prester John* is prototypical in undermining the xenophobia of representative characters, such as Crawfurd, and yet still confirming the danger of the external threat by means of the sheer excess with which that threat is constructed. An educated man (*PJ* 74), Laputa "forecast[s] a day when the negroes would have something to teach the British in the way of civilization" (*PJ* 9). This warning takes the form of both military power and cultural imperialism, the latter of which Laputa discloses through the civility, scholarship, and the "'fineness and nobility'" that make him "'a terrible enemy, but a just one'" (*PJ* 77).

---

[39] For more on this point see my "Buchan and the Pacifists," in Macdonald, *RJB* 91-101.

[40] See also *CG* 35-6.

CHAPTER THREE

INVASIONS, SPYING, CONFLICT

The consolidation of the invasion tale as a distinctive mode of late nineteenth- and early twentieth-century popular writing affords an important context in which Buchan's pre- and First World War thrillers ought to be considered. It is by dint of the alarmism, paranoia, and xenophobia of that tradition that some of the significant contours of the twentieth century thriller, as Buchan inherited the genre in its earliest days, took root. George Chesney's *ur*-text, *The Battle of Dorking*, set the stage in 1871, in a highly suggestive and symbolic account of continental aggression and occupation set in the aftermath of the Franco-Prussian War, and against the backdrop of some of Britain's most pressing political imbroglios of the period: India's uprising in 1857, Irish nationalism (Fenianism), and, most importantly, Anglo-German rivalry. Chesney's text depicts an overly-confident Britain declaring war on a nation it is neither economically nor militarily prepared to resist and by which it is abruptly conquered. *The Battle of Dorking* offered a cultural interpretation of the British homeland, one that focused on urban decadence as metonymic of a national decline figuratively articulated as bacterial rotting. The story, then, also functions in quite another sense, playing on the double meaning of "invasion" as the spread of pathogens to imply that the real site of invasion is not the Home County landscape but Britishness itself, whereupon the signs of a frayed set of values blister through.

Numerous tales of this kind appeared in the wake of Chesney's example.[1] But his emphasis on a perceived hubris at the heart of empire, that impression of imminent decline and fall that later commentators such as Elliott Evans Mills, Arthur Balfour, and, as we have seen, Buchan himself likened to the decay of the Roman Empire, underwent a crucial

---

[1] Joseph S. Meisel gives a good overview of these stories in "The Germans are Coming!: British Fiction of a German Invasion, 1871-1913," *War, Literature, and the Arts* 2: 2 (Fall 1990), 41-79. See also I. F. Clarke's indispensable *Voices Prophesying War: Future Wars, 1763-3749*, 2nd edn (Oxford: Oxford University Press, 1992).

metamorphosis in *The Riddle of the Sands* (1903), by Erskine Childers.[2] In this romance of boating, conspiracy, and derring-do, Childers grafted onto the invasion narrative two key elements: the imperial adventure story's use of liminal geographies, borderlands, and frontiers as sites of personal and national transformation; and the empiricism of the detective novel, which defended a rationalist investigative practice in the fight against criminality. What emerged from these generic shake-ups was a new popular writing attuned to the clandestine operations underpinning turn-of-the-century Anglo-German antagonism (which had been developing since at least as far back as 1860)[3] and deeply informed by the emergent forms of surveillance and military development that antagonism produced and continually reauthorized.[4] Suspenseful and comedic, *The Riddle of the Sands* tells the story of two young men (Carruthers, a civil servant, and Davies, a yachtsman) who, in sailing along the Frisian coast, encounter and prevent a German plot to invade England via the North Sea. In saving the day, it is strongly implied that the Britishness these two figures signify is not just bailed out of perils of which it had not even been aware, but *regenerated* from a debilitated, complacent state to one of watchfulness by dint of the worldview its two protagonists employ; a scepticism, Childers implies, which Edwardian Britain would do well to acknowledge.[5]

During his time as editor of the *Scottish Review* (1906-7) Buchan wrote several articles that passed judgment on some of the central issues

---

[2] See [Elliott Evans Mills], *The Decline and Fall of the British Empire* (Oxford: Alden, [1905]) and Arthur Balfour, *Decadence: Henry Sidgwick Memorial Lecture* (Cambridge: Cambridge University Press, 1908). Note also Buchan's retrospective claim in 1936 that during the pre-war years the world was "arrogant and self-satisfied, but behind all its confidence there was an uneasy sense of impending disaster. The old creeds, both religious and political, were largely in process of dissolution, but we did not realise the fact, and therefore did not look for new foundations" (*CO* 123).

[3] Paul Kennedy, *The Rise of the Anglo-German Antagonism, 1860-1914* (London: Allen & Unwin, 1980).

[4] Good overviews of this historical context can be found in: Jörg Duppler, "Rivals at Sea: British-German naval policies before World War I," in Manfred Görtemaker, ed., *Britain and Germany in the Twentieth-Century* (Oxford: Berg, 2006), 13-29; and Nicholas Hiley, "The Failure of British Espionage against Germany, 1907-1914," *Historical Journal* 26: 4 (December 1983), 867-89, and "The Failure of British Counter-Espionage against Germany, 1907-1914," *Historical Journal* 28: 4 (December 1985), 835-62.

[5] David Trotter is especially good on this point. See his essay "The Politics of Adventure in the Early British Spy Novel," in Wesley K. Wark, ed., *Spy Fiction, Spy Films and Real Intelligence* (London: Frank Cass, 1991), 30-54.

that Chesney and Childers explored in their respective fictions: the organization of the British army, the problems generated by questions of national defence, and the growth of free trade capitalism.[6] But it was in *The Power-House*, serialized by Blackwood in 1913 and published in book form in 1916, that Buchan most successfully began to communicate his views regarding the vulnerabilities around which these issues turned into fictional reality. Inspired by the thrillers of E. Phillips Oppenheim, whom Buchan ambiguously considered his "master in fiction ... the greatest Jewish writer since Isaiah," *The Power-House* lacks the dogmatic tinge of *The Riddle of the Sands*, which in large part was produced by Childers in order to help bring about policy reform.[7] Through the anxious references of its characters to fantasies of evil, ubiquitous German spies (*PH* 13), "defence matters" (*PH* 24), the contingencies of credit finance (*PH* 26), anarchism, and such domestic issues as immigration (*PH* 4) and the British Army's provisions for cavalry-based warfare (*PH* 2), the novel also registers the anxieties of a nation concerned about its own standing in a modern era increasingly characterized by worldwide plotting and global envy.[8]

The Power-House is narrated by Edward Leithen, "a Member of Parliament and of the Bar" (*PH* 23), as he is drawn into a series of cat-and-mouse intrigues when Charles Pitt-Heron, by marriage a relative to Leithen's friend Tommy Deloraine, inexplicably vanishes. This disappearance is gradually explained as an escape to Bokhara in Uzbekistan, a getaway from an association between Pitt-Heron and a "secret organization which went under the name of the Power-House" (*PH* 42), and behind which is the elderly, enigmatic Andrew Lumley, a "pure intelligence, a brain stripped of every shred of humanity" (*PH* 90). Portraying himself as a sleuth, Leithen applies his jurisprudential training to a form of scientific inquiry in which he attempts to locate Pitt-Heron, determine the exact nature of his link to Lumley, and protect the former (and civilization at large) from the latter's nefarious designs. London becomes a danger zone as the façade of everyday life turns criminal, as Leithen gets ever closer to the "dark labyrinths" (*PH* 63) of the Power-House's machinery and previously innocent spaces suddenly become dangerous. Leithen finally learns of Lumley's part in a plot to assassinate Pitt-Heron on the Indian frontier and confronts him in his rooms at the

---

[6] See "Lord Haldane's 'New Model'" (1907), "The Problem of Defence" (1907), and "The Prospects of Free Trade" (1908), in *CC* 3-7, 8-11, 20-2.

[7] Quoted in Lownie, *PC* 137. See also Adam Smith, *JB* 252.

[8] For more on German spy scares during the period, see David French, "Spy Fever in Britain, 1900-1935," *Historical Journal* 21: 2 (June 1978), 355-70.

Albany with an offer to secure his freedom from arrest by leaving
England. The next day, we are led to infer, Lumley dies, ostensibly by his
own hand.

   The Power-House presents London as wild space: elemental,
uncivilized, and perilous. In *The Riddle of the Sands* Childers argued that
Britain ought to pay heed to the instabilities of its European borderlines,
but in *The Power-House* Buchan went one step further in suggesting that
the Imperial metropolitan centre itself was latent with primitive drives and
energies. The following passage, which describes Leithen's anxious
passage through the city (escorted by Chapman, a fellow MP), is apposite:

> [T]here was no sign of trouble till we got into Oxford Street. Then I
> became aware that there were people on these pavements who knew all
> about me. I first noticed it at the mouth of one of those little dark side-
> alleys which run up into mews and small dingy courts. I found myself
> being skilfully edged away from Chapman into the shadow, but I noticed it
> in time and butted my way back to the pavement. I couldn't make out who
> the people were who hustled me. They seemed nondescripts of all sorts,
> but I fancied there were women among them. (*PH* 67-8)

In this extract, London is radically defamiliarized. What once seemed
innocuous and protected has now been infiltrated by enemy agents and
saboteurs. For Leithen's male-centred, totemic worldview, particularly
troubling is the fact that his pursuers include *women*, a hint of the
ubiquitous nature of the conspiracy arrayed against him and a reminder of
the one-sidedness of his ideological coordinates. Oxford Street, the aortic
heart-line of London's economy and the symbolic centre of Imperial
commerce, transforms from busy thoroughfare to potentially barbaric
hinterland. As Leithen says: "It was the homely London I knew so well,
and I was somehow an exile from it. I was being shepherded into a dismal
isolation, which, unless I won help, might mean death" (*PH* 74).

   Through Lumley, Buchan raises the possibility that the quite specific
fears signalled by Leithen's metropolitan experiences are indicative of a
more general sense of contingency, one in which the ostensible
permanence of culture in fact rests upon fibres that, subjected to enough
pressure, might break at any time. In contrast to Leithen's faith in the
tenure of civilization, Lumley offers an anarchic view of society as a
conspiracy, a "'silent compact of comfortable folk to keep up pretences'"
(*PH* 28) that is threatened by "nameless brains" who "now and then
showed their power by some cataclysmic revelation," such as "a sudden
breach between two nations, a blight on a vital crop, a war, a pestilence"
(*PH* 30). In this reading of affairs the key terms are precariousness,

vulnerability, delicacy, and frailty. Whereas Leithen asserts that civilization's key-points are "'strongly held'" (*PH* 27), Lumley sees only "'a multiplicity of small things, all delicate and fragile, and strong only by our tacit agreement not to question them'" (*PH* 27). It is this view that leads him to his infamous account of society as a high-wire balancing act, what Buchan described in the early short story "Fountainblue" (1901) as that "'very narrow line between the warm room and the savage out-of-doors'" (*SS2* 33). "'Reflect,'" Lumley advises, "'and you will find that the foundations are sand. You think that a wall as solid as the earth separates civilization from barbarism. I tell you the division is a thread, a sheet of glass. A touch here, a push there, and you bring back the reign of Saturn'" (*PH* 26). Although Leithen suggests that the "'super-anarchy'" (*PH* 30) Lumley describes here has not, in fact, made any practical headway in the public realm, the latter retorts by arguing that anarchism's overt ineffectiveness is a direct product of the insular disposition of its devotees: "'Civilization wins because it is a world-wide league; its enemies fail because they are parochial. But supposing—'" (*PH* 31). That suggestive, closing hesitation remains unelaborated, but the point is clear: culture is safe so long as its apparent impregnability is taken for granted; the moment anarchism becomes organized is the moment civilization dies.

Mesmerizing, Napoleonic, and possessed of "pale, bright, and curiously wild" eyes that "spoke of wisdom and power as well as of endless vitality" (*PH* 25), Lumley is the classic Buchan villain *and* one of his most interesting psychological studies.[9] Part of this interest stems from Lumley's anticipation of characters such as Graf Otto van Schwabing in *The Thirty-Nine Steps* and *Mr Standfast*, and even Castor, the devilish autocrat of *The Courts of the Morning* (1929).[10] But Lumley is also fascinating as a character in his own right. In a brief episode during Leithen's first meeting with Lumley, the latter reminds him of "a small man of the Professor class" who "conversed fluently but quaintly in English" and was "a Nietzschean and a hot rebel against the established

---

[9] Lumley is compared, and compares himself, to Napoleon on several occasion throughout the text: see *PH* 32, 82, 89, 93. In *Memory Hold-the-Door* Buchan writes that his early reading afforded him a number of prejudices, of which one was a passionate aversion to the French dictator: "I disliked Brutus, Henry VIII, Napoleon (him intensely), most of the 1688 Whigs, all four Georges, and the whole tribe of French revolutionaries except Mirabeau" (*MHD* 41).

[10] In this context, Castor's rejection of his own earlier Napoleonism is significant: "'I have jettisoned my old ambition. I hoped to be a Napoleon to change the shape of the world. Fool that I was! I should only have begun to yawn after it was done, and then somebody would have shot me'" (*CM* 309-10).

order" (*PH* 31), a description that harks back to both the post-Nietzschean Professor from Joseph Conrad's *The Secret Agent* (1907) and to Professor Moriarty from Arthur Conan Doyle's Sherlock Holmes stories.[11] Likewise, in *The Power-House*, Lumley's Nietzschean politics are both rhetorically startling and preposterously extreme to the authorities they antagonize. *Übermensch* (of a sort) Lumley may think himself to be, but to Leithen he remains a "bland superman" (*PH* 38), a ruling both enforced by textual suppression and closure (Lumley is killed off), and by Leithen's final dismissal of Lumley's beliefs: "I could dimly imagine what his death meant to the hosts who had worked blindly at his discretion. He was a Napoleon who left no Marshals behind him. From the Power-House came no wreaths, or newspaper tributes, but I knew that it had lost its power" (*PH* 93).

Through Lumley, *The Power-House* interrogates the capacity of professional forms of identity both to exemplify individual aptitudes and to contend with particular social hazards. During their initial meeting, Leithen can only take a guess at Lumley's chosen vocation, supposing him to be either "a retired Oxford don, or one of the higher civil servants, or perhaps some official of the British Museum" (*PH* 24), but almost immediately thereafter, as Leithen confesses, "[a]ll my theories vanished, for I could not believe that my host had ever followed any profession. If he had, he would have been at the head of it, and the world would have been familiar with his features" (*PH* 25). At that same meeting Lumley himself inquires of Leithen as to why the latter chose the profession of the Bar, and, later in the text, says that if his view of civilization as perennially at risk is, in fact, true, then Leithen's account of lawyers as the "'cement of civilization'" (*PH* 25) is woefully inadequate to the dangers at hand. "'If there is an atom of truth in my fancies,'" Lumley warns, "'your task is far bigger than you thought. You are not defending an easy case, but fighting in a contest where the issues are still doubtful'" (*PH* 32-3). Moreover, Leithen's allies echo Lumley's doubts. Near the start of the novel, for instance, Tommy Deloraine asserts that out of his friends not one is following their proper trade (*PH* 2), and when Leithen learns of

---

[11] This Holmesian echo is discussed in John Towner, "Thrillers and the roots of civilisation," *John Buchan Journal* 20 (Spring 1999), 23-32, at 26. There is a direct link through the Nietzschean context to what we have already seen as Buchan's own life history. Having read Nietzsche's works with great interest at Oxford, Buchan later distanced himself from the German philosopher's reading of modernity. Although in "Professor Saintsbury and European Literature" (1907) he admitted to being an admirer of Nietzsche's literary qualities, Buchan remained opposed to "the madness of his conclusions" (*CC* 220).

Deloraine's imminent departure for the Russian principality of Muscovy, even he himself reflects: "I remember the occasion [...] for it was one of the few on which I have had a pang of dissatisfaction with the calling I had chosen" (*PH* 7). As the novel progresses Leithen's frustration with his professional status is sublimated in his desire to move beyond jurisprudence onto the front line of sleuth-craft; as Leithen states, "every man at the bottom of his heart believes that he is a born detective" (*PH* 13). The point here is not that Leithen *becomes* a detective, but that his decisions begin to be filtered through the empirical thought processes upon which criminal investigation stands.[12]

Buchan's focus on the figure of the detective is as much a generic comment as it is a question of narrative subject. For in signalling the appropriateness of detective-work in dealing with the dangers of a metropolis as precarious, as *adventurous* as any far-flung imperial frontier, *The Power-House* brings the formal metamorphosis begun by Childers to its logical end-point: a detective story in which the metropolis *becomes* the frontier. Significantly, *The Power-House* ends in a complex, generically self-reflexive nod towards this development:

> 'I have had the time of my life,' [Tommy] said. 'It was like a chapter out of the Arabian Nights with a dash of Fenimore Cooper. I feel as if I had lived years since I left England in May. While you have been sitting among your musty papers we have been riding like mosstroopers and seeing men die. Come and dine tonight and hear about our adventures. I can't tell you the full story, for I don't know it, but there is enough to curl your hair.'
>
> Then I achieved my first and last score at the expense of Tommy Deloraine.
>
> 'No,' I said, 'you will dine with me instead, and *I* will tell you the full story. All the papers on the subject are over there in my safe.' (*PH* 94-5)

Despite Deloraine's risk-taking away from home, the real adventurer here, and thus the only fully-informed story-teller, is Leithen. Deloraine's reputation for Equatorial exploits (*PH* 2) is mirrored no less in the escapades Leithen has endured in London. The world's dangers are no longer "out there" but "here," at home. Leithen's battles with Lumley have been just as romantically Cooperian and as exotic as Deloraine's adventures in Muscovy, if not more so, for, in his fight with the lord of the Power-House, Leithen has acquired the broader self-knowledge and experienced the truer jeopardy. The notes in Leithen's safe are the

---

[12] In this regard, Leithen's account of his analyses in the following passage is instructive: "That night I went carefully over every item in the evidence to try and decide on my next step. I had got to find out more about my enemies" (*PH* 38-9).

objective correlative to a multi-layered moment of generic metamorphosis, one that rammed the thriller form itself into undiscovered territories.

In *The Thirty-Nine Steps* Buchan firmed up the contours of this fresh kind of writing. Written between July and December 1914, it was serialized in *The All-Story Weekly* in June and July 1915, followed by *Blackwood's Magazine* in installments from July to September of that year (Macdonald, *CMF* 169). It was published by Blackwood's in October 1915, selling 25,000 copies within three months (Lownie, *PC* 119-20). Like *The Power-House*, *The Thirty-Nine Steps* signals its own generic status in referencing H. Rider Haggard (imperial adventure) and Arthur Conan Doyle (detective story) as literary exemplars (*TNS* 33). This novel, Buchan's strategy pronounces, is a modern rephrasing of the textual traditions their writing epitomizes. *The Thirty-Nine Steps* is a "double-flight" narrative in which its protagonist, Richard Hannay, goes on the run, both from a sinister cabal (*Der schwarze Stein*; "The Black Stone") and the authorities, after he is falsely implicated in the murder of an American spy, Franklin P. Scudder. At first Hannay is led to believe that a conspiracy is afoot to throw Europe into war by assassinating the Greek Premier, but by deciphering Scudder's code-book Hannay discovers that the real plot is a German effort to obtain the disposition of the British Home Fleet, mine Britain's coastline, and destroy its naval defence forces. Hannay's flight takes him from the centre of London to the Scots Moors and back again while he is pursued both on foot and from the skies, ending in a scene on the Kentish coast where he defies the Black Stone, unravels their plans, and, befitting the hero he has by then become, saves the day for all concerned.

The dominant way of reading *The Thirty-Nine Steps* (about which more in my concluding chapter) has been to pin it down as the "first" or archetypal spy thriller.[13] Such a reading has clear genealogical advantages, but a more precise description would be to see it as a key production in a developing corpus of popular espionage narratives, a work in which (as we will see in my concluding chapter) the gentlemanly ethics and amateurism of a Leithen begin to shift into the colder, more professional codes of the secret agent even as that figure was finding its own institutional identity in the nascent British Secret Service. *The Thirty-Nine Steps* ought to be read

---

[13] A somewhat curious formulation of this view is provided by LeRoy Panek: "Buchan took the spy novel out of the hands of innocuous romancers like Oppenheim and gave it sinew and meaning. Regardless of chronology or irrelevant 'firsts,' Buchan started the modern spy novel, and in its best manifestations the spy novel returns to him" (*The Special Branch: The British Spy Novel, 1890-1980* (Bowling Green, OH: Bowling Green University Popular Press, 1981), 66).

as a text responded to and taken up by such later figures as Graham Greene and Eric Ambler in various ways that enabled the variegated tradition we now label "the spy thriller" to come into being. Any discussion about Buchan's "firstness" here is thus displaced by a broader emphasis on transitivity. *The Thirty-Nine Steps* is not about professional spies, as such, but about the conditioned identities out of which professional spying emerged. In this respect, Hannay's "becoming" is as much the subject of *The Thirty-Nine Steps* as is the crisis the text apprehensively describes. We are told from the outset that he is thirty-seven years old, is Scottish by birth, and, since the age of six, has resided in Southern Rhodesia (now Zimbabwe), where he made a small fortune for himself in the mining trade (*TNS* 7). Hannay fought in the Matabele War (*TNS* 19), and was an intelligence officer during the Boer War (*TNS* 25). His status as a gentleman is confirmed by his Clubland affiliations (*TNS* 8), with its public school underpinnings, and by certain class markings, such as his apartment in Langham Place in the centre of London, his butler, and his Newboltian habit of explaining trauma in terms of game-playing and sportsmanship.[14] If these elements remain more or less in place come the novel's close, then what changes as it proceeds is Hannay's attitude towards them. As he falls into an increasingly alienated world deeply informed by the silent and clandestine, his "journey" is revealed as both a literal movement through the British mainland and a mending of his previously tarnished faith in Britain's ideological institutions, one that revitalizes both his own psyche and, in a symbolic sense, the political standing of the homeland itself.

David Trotter's view of *The Thirty-Nine Steps* as "a wonderfully economical recapitulation of the form developed by Oppenheim and others" should alert us to the deep indebtedness of Buchan's writing to its precursors, but it also ought to remind us of its shaping by the invasion story tradition through which those same precursors were formed.[15] One of the most elementary anxieties in *The Thirty-Nine Steps* is the issue of national defence. As Hannay comes to learn, the real conspiracy at work here is a German plot to lull the British authorities into a false sense of security so that Hannay's "Old Country" (*TNS* 7) can be attacked: "Honey and fair speeches, and then a stroke in the dark. While we were talking

---

[14] For more on the presence of "Newbolt Man" in British popular literature, see Patrick Howarth, *Play Up and Play the Game: The Heroes of Popular Fiction* (London: Eyre Methuen, 1973).

[15] David Trotter, *Paranoid Modernism: Literary Experiment, Psychosis, and the Professionalization of English Society* (Oxford: Oxford University Press, 2001), 144.

about the goodwill and good intentions of Germany our coast would be silently ringed with mines, and submarines would be waiting for every battleship" (*TNS* 38).[16] But, as Hannay theorizes, the real catastrophe is not only attack but *subjugation*, an end result only possible if German jackboots stand on British soil. Such a view is only reinforced by Hannay's unsympathetic response to the naïve objections of Sir Harry Bullivant, "the radical candidate," who dismisses the "German menace" as a Rightist smokescreen designed "to cheat the poor of their rights and keep back the great flood of social reform," and campaigns for a reduction of the British Navy as proof of Britain's "good faith" (*TNS* 44) in the perilous continuum of Anglo-German relations during this period. Hannay averts invasion, but these references to images of a conquered homeland stand as symptoms of fears that had lingered on from the turn of the century, and which were quite obviously about to be thrown centre stage with the onset of world war.[17]

One indication of the significance of Hannay's accomplishment in preventing a German invasion of England in *The Thirty-Nine Steps* is the theological flavour Buchan imparts to his activities. There is a clear parallel in the very title of *The Thirty-Nine Steps* with the Thirty-Nine Articles of the Anglican Church, thus superimposing onto Hannay's doings Buchan's Calvinist reading of modernity as necessitating a continual striving towards Faith. Early on, Hannay describes London as a "God-forgotten metropolis" (*TNS* 15), and shortly after Scudder is killed Hannay describes himself as "a God-forgotten fool" (*TNS* 22). References to divine intervention are plentiful here: Hannay thanks Providence for bringing him into Bullivant's company (*TNS* 43), thus rescuing him from the police; Hannay refers to a "big knot of hill" which he chooses as a "sanctuary" (*TNS* 48); and he is even cared for by the plucky wife of a herdsman, who tends Hannay "like a true Samaritan" (*TNS* 73). Prayer is

---

[16] Buchan discussed the issue of submarine mines in "The Fiasco of the Hague Conference" (1907). See *CC* 348-9.

[17] But note Frank McDonough's important recent claim that during the Edwardian period "the public attitudes of Conservatives towards the key aspects of Anglo-German relations showed a high level of public restraint and a marked absence of open hostility. Scaremongering against Germany in public [was] the preserve of ultra right-wing 'outcasts' on the 'radical right' of the party, without any real influence over the Conservative leadership. Indeed, the so-called radical right was more a 'loony right' who had a very limited impact in persuading the Conservative leadership to adopt a more strident Germanophobic approach" (*The Conservative Party and Anglo-German Relations, 1905-1914* (Basingstoke: Palgrave Macmillan, 2007), 138).

an important component of Hannay's skill-set, such as when he prays that
the roadman whose clothes he borrows for a disguise will be secure before
Hannay's "friends" (his hunters) arrive on the scene (*TNS* 51). The bald
archaeologist's mansion is depicted by Hannay as an "accursed dwelling"
(*TNS* 71), an image echoed in one of Hannay's more intriguing self-
descriptions: "Contrary to general belief, I was not a murderer, but I had
become an unholy liar, a shameless impostor, and a highway-man with a
marked taste for expensive motor-cars" (*TNS* 56). That Buchan so
painstakingly installs these religious overtones in *The Thirty-Nine Steps*
makes it tempting to see in Hannay's final view of his experiences as his
"best service" (*TNS* 111) an articulation of an expressly *spiritual* service to
a God he has spent the majority of the narrative in figuratively relocating.
In *The Thirty-Nine Steps*, coming in from the cold seems also to be
coming back into the flock.[18]

John Milton's presence in *The Thirty-Nine Steps*, through a telling
allusion to his epic poem *Paradise Lost*, hints at a mingling of the
Christian with the pagan which results in a reinforcement of the sacred.
Shortly before his discovery of the Black Stone's true intentions, Hannay
overhears the innkeeper allude to a short passage from Book II of Milton's
religious epic: "*As when a Gryphon through the wilderness* | *With wingéd
step, o'er hill and moory dale* | *Pursues the Arimaspian*" (*TNS* 31). The
passage in question is from a sequence describing Satan's exit from Hell
into Chaos, in which he is compared to the flying gryphons continually
warring against the cyclopean Arimaspians of Scythia. In addition to
adding mythological detail to the spatial qualities of *The Thirty-Nine
Steps*, this reference to *Paradise Lost* implicitly confers a twofold
mythological-theological significance on both Hannay's entanglements
and the political discoveries they facilitate. The allusion suggests that the
monocular, "Arimaspian" Hannay's flight from the Germans pursuing him
in a gryphon-like, "infernal aeroplane" (*TNS* 40) signifies a Miltonian
theology, one in which Hannay is not just caught up in a contest between
Good and Evil but is participating in a deeper negotiation with the nature
of religious identity. At the same time, the allusion gives an epiphanic
substance to that moment of revelation in which Hannay learns the true
designs of the Black Stone by decoding Scudder's note-book, a text
Hannay reads "with a whitish face and fingers that drummed on the table"

---

[18] David Daniell suggests that, in the transition from *The Power-House* to *The
Thirty-Nine Steps*, "Buchan comes back to modern London deliberately coasting
along the very edge of the frontier between the real and the unreal, the Calvinist-
cum-Platonist consciousness of other worlds impinging on our own" (*The
Interpreter's House*, 132).

(*TNS* 34). In this context, the movement from monocularity to double-sightedness (from ignorance to a certain level of insight) that act of reading enables moves Hannay a footstep closer to a final knowledge (a confirmation of the correctness of Scudder's theories that comes only in the text's ending chapter) that is, in turn, related to the divine. "I must show a sign," Hannay knows, "some token in proof, and *Heaven* knew what that could be" (*TNS* 39, my emphasis).

Buchan's use of theology in describing Hannay's enemies was a potentially explosive strategy in the Germanophobic climate of 1915. To speak of the Black Stone's leader as "weird and devilish" (*TNS* 64) and an "infernal antiquarian" (*TNS* 101), or to depict the faction itself as "those devilish Germans" (*TNS* 72), is to draw upon a discriminatory vocabulary in which difference is silently reinforced through politicized sinfulness. That said, wartime stereotyping of "Huns" and "the Boche" is noticeably absent from *The Thirty-Nine Steps*. After all, the text overwhelmingly is a war book, begun after the Great War had got under way and (a point infrequently acknowledged) narrated from a post-1914 perspective, one that is concerned not just with the threat of war but also the discursive contours through which the War itself was conducted and explained.[19] In this sense, Buchan's avoidance of a sweeping generalization of Germany as menacingly "other" is significant, for it situates him in a notable company of careful thinkers who refused to discriminate against the German people purely on the basis of race or nationality. The kind of claim made in May 1915 by H. G. Wells that "[n]othing can better serve the purpose of our enemies, nothing can inflict worse injuries upon humanity at large, than to hold each and every German accountable for the offences of the German Government" trickles into *The Thirty-Nine Steps* through an open signalling of Hannay's German affiliations.[20] As Hannay himself notes near the start of his escapades: "I had half an idea at first to be a German tourist, for my father had had German partners, and I had been brought up to speak the tongue pretty fluently, not to mention having put in three years prospecting for copper in German Damaraland" (*TNS* 21). Hannay's know-how with the German language helps him during an escape, and it gives him insights into the bald archaeologist's conversations

---

[19] Hannay's closing words—"Three weeks later, as all the world knows, we went to war. I joined the New Army the first week, and owing to my Matabele experience got a captain's commission straight off. But I had done my best service, I think, before I put on khaki" (*TNS* 111)—confirm the text as being reported from a moment in time *after* the War has started.
[20] *The Correspondence of H. G. Wells: Volume 2, 1904-1918*, ed. David C. Smith (London: Pickering & Chatto, 1998), 420.

that he would not otherwise have had. In this sense, Buchan resists those easy oppositions between the Tommy and an exaggeratedly brutish enemy produced by such testimonies as the Bryce Report in 1915.

Buchan returned to the issue of anti-German sentiment in several of the non-fictional works he wrote during the War. In his December 1915 speech for Francis Younghusband's "Fight for Right" movement (published as the pamphlet *The Purpose of War* in 1916), Buchan took Germany to task for its expansionism, militarism, and race pride, and he attributed its coldness towards the ideals of other nations and its conquest-lust to a form of vulgar materialism. But that same speech made it clear that Buchan was criticizing a nation the majority of which, he thought, had succumbed to ruling-class demagoguery. In this view, the German enemy was not the ordinary German citizen or combatant, but the Establishment which had led such individuals astray: "Germany took immense pains to prove to the world that she was the aggrieved and not the aggressor, that she was engaged in a war of legitimate self-defence, and all the rest of it. It rang very false, because the deeds, and the speeches, and the writings of the first months give it the lie. But it convinced the German people and the German army."[21] Other pamphlets, such as *The Future of the War* (1916), emphasized the courage of the ordinary German soldier, although here Buchan insisted upon the superiority of Allied "corporate" fortitude over its German equivalent.[22] Like many of his peers—including the Ford Madox Hueffer [Ford] of such texts as *When Blood is their Argument* (1915) and *Between St Dennis and St George* (1915)—Buchan rejected Prussianism and *Kultur* as deeply problematic forms of civilization. He outlined Prussianism in particular in his majestic *Nelson's History of the Great War* as having come from the same stock as Bolshevism: "Both unduly simplified the world, both were without sense of history, both would substitute for the rich and organic variousness of life a harsh mechanism. [...] Each was a devotee of *Machtpolitik*; each sought, in defiance of right and justice, to impose its theories on the world by force."[23]

Greenmantle (1916), the sequel to *The Thirty-Nine Steps*, explores the nuances of Anglo-German relations in detail. Its plot is one of Buchan's finest. Opening some eighteen months after the end of *The Thirty-Nine Steps*, Hannay is now "an obscure Major of the New Army" (*G* 7-8) in line for the command of a battalion, but most of the narrative is concerned not

---

[21] Buchan, *The Purpose of War* (London: Dent, 1916), 6.

[22] Buchan, *The Future of the War* (London: Boyle, 1916), 8.

[23] Buchan, *Nelson's History of the War*, 24 vols. (London: Nelson, 1915-1919), vol. 21 (1918), 173.

with the Front but with Hannay's undercover doings in Europe and the
Middle East. Accompanied by his friends Sandy Arbuthnot, John S.
Blenkiron, and Peter Pienaar, Hannay travels from Holland to the Battle of
Erzerum in Turkey as he attempts to foil a German plot to inflame Islam
against Christianity. A colourful cast of characters awaits them, among
others: the vicious Colonel Ulric von Stumm; Hilda von Einem, "The
Lady of the Mantilla" with an "inscrutable smile and devouring eyes" (*G*
173); Gaudian, a likeable German officer; and even the Kaiser himself,
Emperor Wilhelm II. Hannay has only three bizarre clues upon which to
proceed: the words "Kasredin," "cancer," and "v. I." As with his eventual
decoding of Scudder's cipher in *The Thirty-Nine Steps*, Hannay unravels
their significance and learns that Germany plans to facilitate the return of
the Mohammedan prophet Greenmantle, a man with sufficient influence to
bring Islam's "'fighting creed'" (*G* 12) to the West. When Greenmantle
suddenly dies, Einem attempts to replace him with Arbuthnot, with whom
she has fallen in love. But, in a great *coup*, Arbuthnot turns the tables on
his German antagonists by switching sides at a crucial moment in the
skirmish for the citadel of Kara Gubek, shortly before the triumphant
Russian cavalry charge and Allied victory. As Priya Satia writes,
"[p]ainting for the first time on such a vast geographical canvas, Buchan
also liberally exploited the landscape's biblical resonances, not least with
the apotheosis at the [novel's] climax: the image of the prophet Sandy
leading the Russians to Erzerum."[24]

Einem and Stumm are caricatural figures who, through their use of
mesmerism and pugilism respectively, undergird an apocalyptic monism—
a "monstrous bloody Juggernaut that was crushing the life out of the little
heroic nations" (*G* 117)—that has as its objective the diminution of
"'civilisation to a featureless monotony'" so that Germany can govern its
"'inanimate corpse'" (*G* 184). Einem is presented as a female version of
the *Ubermensch* (*G* 184), something "demonic" from beyond the earthly
domain. Stumm is both a physical stereotype—a "perfect mountain of a
fellow, six and half feet if he was an inch, with shoulders on him like a
shorthorn bull" (*G* 50)—somewhat in the guise of the Teutons in the
propaganda postcards of Alberto Martini and Henri Zislin. For Hannay at
least, he is a disquietingly "alternative" military man. In spite of the
muscle and the brawn, Stumm's menace lies not in brute physicality but in
the less tolerable realm of daintiness, what Hannay later terms the
"Chinese language" (*G* 170) of feminine chic and elegance. Disguised as

---

[24] Priya Satia, *Spies in Arabia: The Great War and the Cultural Foundations of
Britain's Covert Empire in the Middle East* (Oxford: Oxford University Press,
2008), 88.

Cornelius Brandt, a Boer sympathetic to Germany, Hannay is taken to Stumm's castle where he initially mistakes the Colonel's private quarters for "a woman's drawing-room" (*G* 79). However, for Hannay the truth is more distressing: "There had never been a woman's hand in that place. It was the room of a man who had a passion for frippery, who had a perverted taste for soft delicate things. It was the complement to his bluff brutality. I began to see the queer other side to my host, that evil side which gossip had spoken of as not unknown in the German army" (*G* 79). While it is ambiguous as to whether or not Stumm ultimately represents a homosexual Other here, the passage just quoted makes it clear that, to Hannay, Stumm signifies a kind of puissant but inadmissible (and perhaps misperceived) effeminacy, one that, like Hannay's view of Einem's masculinized womanliness, must be resisted if not shunned.[25]

Hannay's response to these two figures is not necessarily Buchan's. There is a closeness between Buchan and Hannay, but *Greenmantle* goes to some lengths to insist on the constructedness of Hannay's point of view, a perspective that colours all the descriptions of other characters in the novel, and which, like the other Hannay stories, can be traced back to the text's first-person mode of narration. Indeed, *Greenmantle* reveals that the alterity of both Einem and Stumm is largely a product of the manner in which Hannay and his associates inevitably perceive them through their own ideological blinkers. Einem and Stumm threaten as manifestations of atypical forms of gender identity, but they do so only insofar as they call into question the epistemological certainties of *Greenmantle*'s heroes, a move that is as generic as it is thematic.[26] As in *The Thirty-Nine Steps*, Hannay's mission is quite obviously a quest to sift through and identify certain kinds of information (clues, leads, maps, bodily gestures) which will ultimately bring about victory, but from *Greenmantle*'s dedicatory page onwards the world of male brotherhood, intimacy, and fellowship as known to Hannay from his ongoing service in Kitchener's Army is signalled as constituting his primary locus of meaning. From this angle, Einem and Stumm violate Hannay's own categories of intellection—his *experience*—inasmuch as they contravene the prejudices afforded to him by an all-male system of military kinship. Thus, while Blenkiron asserts that Einem's threat lies principally in abomination, Hannay recognizes her

---

[25] See Macdonald, *CMF* 46 for further commentary on this episode. See also Colin Storer, "'The German of caricature, the real Geman, the fellow we were up against': German Stereotypes in John Buchan's *Greenmantle*," *Journal of European Studies* 39: 1 (2009), 36-57.
[26] Thomas Richards, *The Imperial Archive: Knowledge and the Fantasy of Empire* (London: Verso, 1993), 114-15.

as from beyond the empirical realm made available to him through the ideological coordinates produced by his soldiering: "'Mad and bad,' Blenkiron had called her, 'but principally bad.' I did not think they were the proper terms, for they belonged to the narrow world of our *common experience*. This was something beyond and above it, as a cyclone or an earthquake is outside the decent routine of nature" (*G* 173, my emphasis).[27] Likewise, of Stumm Hannay states: "He was a new thing in my *experience* and I didn't like it" (*G* 79, my emphasis). In the same fashion as the monsters and ghouls of the *fin de siècle* gothic romances by which *Greenmantle* is clearly influenced, the dangers posed by Einem and Stumm lie in their inability to be pigeonholed into strictly-defined cognitive parameters.[28]

This exaggerated otherness is counter-balanced by the novel's clear sympathy towards Germany's traditions, individual personages, and the sufferings of its ordinary citizens during the First World War. Hannay refers to Germany as "a civilised country full of roads and railways" (*G* 92), and he describes the German officer Gaudian as "clearly a good fellow" (*G* 67) who "was about the greatest living authority on tropical construction" (*G* 64). Hannay takes refuge in a "desperately poor" (*G* 99) family dwelling near the river Danube populated by a widow whose face, unlike the liberal allowance allotted to soldiers' wives in England at that time, "had the skin stretched tight over the bones and that transparency which means underfeeding" (*G* 99). There is a hint in Hannay's view of the sailors with whom he travels in disguise on the Essen barges as "mostly Frisians, slow-spoken, sandy-haired lads, very like the breed you strike on the Essex coast" (*G* 108) of a racial proximity that the xenophobic politics of the Anglo-German antagonism would have denied. The most startling sympathy in the text is its infamous, and, for the period, extraordinarily audacious, view of the Kaiser as "a human being who, unlike Stumm and his kind, had the power of laying himself alongside other men" (*G* 76-7). Unlike the satirical postcard imagery of the Kaiser attempting to devour the world, this Kaiser is a deeply troubled self: "this man, the chief of a nation of Stumms, paid the price in war for the gifts that had made him successful in peace. He had imagination and nerves, and the one was white hot and the others were quivering. I would not have been in his shoes for the throne of the Universe" (*G* 77).

---

[27] But note that this insight of Hannay's finds an echo in Blenkiron's view of Einem as a "'very *different* proposition'" (*G* 49, my emphasis).

[28] Patrick Brantlinger discusses this line of influence in *Rule of Darkness: British Literature and Imperialism, 1830-1914* (Ithaca: Cornell University Press, 1988), 227.

Buchan's wartime thrillers and the various short stories and poems he wrote between 1914 and 1918 should not obscure just how many non-fictional texts he produced during that same period. The narrator figure in *Huntingtower* claims that "[t]he military historian must often make shift to write of battles with slender data, but he can pad out his deficiencies by learned parallels" (*H* 171). Buchan's war histories are filled with such parallels, but they neither compensate for intellectual defects nor suppress any kind of ignorance as to figures. All are erudite, scholarly volumes that astonish with their breadth and range of reference no less so than with their statistical grasp. Buchan's input to the *Nelson's History* (1915-19) totalled a massive twenty-four volumes, each running to around 50,000 words, and each approximately taking between thirty and sixty days to complete. Between August 1914 and March 1915 Buchan edited and wrote a number of articles for *The War*, a weekly magazine again published by Nelson's, and he was the author of several specialized war histories such as *Britain's War by Land* (1915), *The Achievement of France* (1915), *The Battle of Jutland* (1916), *The British Front in the West, November 1916* (1916), *The Battle of the Somme, First Phase* (1916), *The British Front in the West, February 1917* (1917), *The Battle of the Somme, Second Phase* (1917). In 1915 Buchan worked for *The Times* and *The Daily News* as a war correspondent, and all this on top of working for the government in a wide variety of roles: an officer in the Intelligence Corps (1915), a Staff Captain at GHQ under General Haig (mid-1916), and the Director of the Department of Information in London (late 1916-18).[29] Buchan's bewilderingly detailed knowledge of the War's key events and personalities imparts a cornucopia of period detail to *Greenmantle* in particular, with its dense account of Turkey's involvement in contemporary German politics, but it is in *Mr Standfast* (written between 1917 and 1918, published in 1919) that Buchan most imaginatively engaged with the War, its horrors, and its creation of private and public estrangements.[30]

This is not to claim that he steered clear of such issues in his non-fictional texts. On the contrary, the *Nelson's History* is candid in its

---

[29] This paragraph is indebted to Kate Macdonald's comprehensive summary of Buchan's non-fictional wartime writing in "Translating Propaganda: John Buchan's Writing During the First World War," in Mary Hammond and Shafquat Towheed, eds, *Publishing in the First World War: Essays in Book History* (Basingstoke: Palgrave Macmillan, 2007), 181-201.

[30] See Kate Macdonald's "Introduction" to the Oxford World's Classics edition of *Greenmantle*, and the *John Buchan Journal*'s *Greenmantle* issue: *John Buchan Journal* 36 (Spring 2007).

presentation of wartime tensions, loss of life, and strategic misjudgements.[31] However, in *Mr Standfast* Buchan was able to describe these concerns in modes unsuitable for journalistic and historiographic discourses. It is in many ways Buchan's most ingenious work of literature, uniting an extended adventure narrative with an account of the Battle of Amiens, articulating both through a symbolic infrastructure borrowed from John Bunyan's *The Pilgrim's Progress* (1678). The novel sees Hannay, Pienaar, and Blenkiron return to action, and it reintroduces Graf Otto von Schwabing at first disguised as the Satanic Moxon Ivery, who is described as "like a poison gas that hung in the air and got into unexpected crannies and that you couldn't fight in an upstanding way" (*MS* 91), a description that anticipates his plan to deploy anthrax poison gas on the Allied lines (*MS* 193).[32] The novel documents Garden City socialism and the labour unrest of the Red Clyde in Glasgow, and it engages with pacifism and conscientious objection, presenting in the character of Launcelot Wake not just a sympathetic portrayal of an objectionism with which Buchan in principle disagreed, but a humanized view that went against the familiar stereotypes of objectors as cowards, weaklings, or, at worst, "un-men." Wake is anything but typecast. Leithen contends in *The Power-House* that "[t]he most pacific fellow on earth can be gingered into pugnacity" (*PH* 48), and while a kind of belligerence is, in certain respects, true of Wake, his desire to fight for the Allied cause come the novel's end signals a genuine resistance to German militarism, an act of repudiation in which pacifism still retains a valid identity.

Pacifism is in many respects the key discourse of *Mr Standfast*. In this regard, the novel forms a central part of Buchan's broader antipathy to the wastefulness of conflict, what he referred to in "The Shut Door" (1926) as "the preposterous waste of war" (*SS3* 70). At the start of the twentieth century, as we saw in the previous chapter, Buchan was opposed to pacifism, but as he lived through the Great War his views gradually came to change. By 1919 Buchan was able to provide a more detailed assessment of the pacifist cause, and he had become sympathetic to the sufferings of individual pacifists and pacifist groups which he felt had been victimized by the Establishment. This led, for example, to his

---

[31] Keith Grieves, "*Nelson's History of the War*: John Buchan as a Contemporary Military Historian, 1915-1922," *Journal of Contemporary History* 28: 3 (July 1993), 533-51.
[32] Note that in *The Courts of the Morning* Castor is described as descending upon the people of Olifa and vanishing "as suddenly as a river mist" (*CM* 37). In this sense both Ivery and Castor threaten insofar as they inhabit, in different ways, nebulous, liminal identities.

qualified support for the sculptor Jacob Epstein's pleas for release from
military service in 1917, and in 1918 Buchan lent his name to a letter
written by the No-Conscription Fellowship to the Prime Minister David
Lloyd George that called for the release of the remaining 1,500
conscientious objectors who had yet to be released from British prisons.[33]
Mr Standfast, in turn, clearly states this refined perspective. With its
descriptions of the community at Biggleswick, the Red Clyde, and Wake,
it shows the diversity of pacifist politics and shows the range of spaces
that generate them; it refuses the typecasting of objectors as degenerates
by portraying them as complex selves motivated by disparate psychologies;
and if it does not assent to pacifist values it holds a somewhat equivalent
view to Herbert Asquith's claim that non-combatants could bear
responsibilities that exposed them "to the very same risks as those who go
into the trenches to man the guns and use the rifles."[34] This last point is
made emphatically in the text by dint of Wake's job as a flank runner: "He
knew nothing of military affairs before," Hannay says, "but he got the
hang of this rough-and-tumble fighting as if he had been born for it. He
never fired a shot; he carried no arms; the only weapons he used were his
brains. And they were the best conceivable" (*MS* 308).

Mr Standfast's emphasis on pacifist forms of identity is inseparable
from its account of religious subjectivity, in particular its account of the
self-sacrifice of Peter Pienaar as a form of selfless and self-directed
violence that aids in ending the larger violence of the Great War through
fraternal love. Throughout *Mr Standfast* it is implied that Allied victory is
possible only insofar as it will entail the sacrifice of Hannay's oldest friend
and mentor, Pienaar. An early reference to him as a "Christian martyr"
(*MS* 14), followed by references to his own death in his letters to Hannay,
and Mary Lamington's suspicion that the adventures of Good will require
a "sacrifice to be made ... the best of us" (*MS* 218), mark him out as a
necessary casualty of war. And perish he does, immolating himself in an
aerial collision with a spotter plane piloted by the German air ace Lensch
(a thinly-disguised Baron von Richthofen) before he can exploit
intelligence regarding a weak point in the Allied line (*MS* 330). Like
Christ sacrificing himself on the cross to save humankind, Pienaar's
renunciation of his own existence is a divinely-sanctioned feat of love for

---

[33] Robert Ferguson, *The Short Sharp Life of T. E. Hulme* (London: Allen Lane,
2002), 256; June Rose, *Daemons and Angels: A Life of Jacob Epstein* (London:
Constable, 2002), 105-10; David Boulton *Objection Overruled* (London:
MacGibbon, 1967), 281.
[34] Quoted in John Rae, *Conscience and Politics* (London: Oxford University Press,
1970), 35.

others: "'[Pienaar] says God has some work for him to do'" (*MS* 322),
says Archie Margolin. Unlike the infernal Ivery, the man "'as cruel as a
snake and as deep as hell'" (*MS* 45), as Blenkiron describes him, an
angelic Pienaar lays down his life for the greater good, resulting in a form
of self-sacrifice that clearly admixes both the sacrificial urge to avenge the
killing of others and the antisacrificial incentive in which, through taking
his own life, the war may be brought that fraction closer to its long-hoped-
for end.[35]

It is clear that Pienaar's literal and symbolic journey upwards into the
sky is meant to be understood as an escape from earthly pressures and
concerns that facilitate a quasi-divine transcendence, an individual
regeneration of Pienaar himself from the man with a "withered leg" (*MS*
291), fractured in an earlier battle with Lensch, to heaven-bound warrior.
Although Pienaar regains much of his strength in the aftermath of his
disablement, he remains a "grizzled cripple" (*MS* 227), depressed by his
affliction and unsure of both his physical and psychological status as a
man: "many a great yarn we spun in the long evenings," remarks Hannay
of time shared with Pienaar during the latter's recuperation, "but I always
went to bed with a sore heart. The longing in his eyes was too urgent,
longing not for old days or far countries, but for the health and strength
which had once been his pride" (*MS* 229). John Galsworthy wrote of
dismemberment in *The Queen's Gift Book* (1915), to which Buchan was a
contributor, that "it is the spirit of a man that suffers when he can no
longer express the bounding energy within him."[36] Likewise, stripped of
his virility by this lack of "bounding energy," Pienaar falls into
decrepitude. "He was so frail and so poor," Hannay observes, "for he had
never had anything in the world but his bodily fitness, and he had lost that
now. And remember he had lost it after some months of glittering
happiness, for in the air he had found the element for which he had been
born" (*MS* 230).

Turning to religion, Pienaar finds a way both to stave off his
depression and a pathway to individual and collective regeneration
through a symbolic re-manning of himself. Pienaar's stoicism prompts
Hannay to keep himself at a renewed level of bodily fitness (*MS* 232), and
it gives back to Pienaar a kind of mental fitness enabling him to bear what

---

[35] For an exemplary discussion of sacrifice, self-sacrifice, and anti-sacrifice during
the Great War, see Allen J. Frantzen, *Bloody Good: Chivalry, Sacrifice, and the
Great War* (Chicago: University of Chicago Press, 2004).
[36] *The Queen's Gift Book: In aid of Queen Mary's Convalescent Auxiliary
Hospitals for Soldiers and Sailors who have lost their limbs in the War*, introd.
John Galsworthy (London: Hodder and Staughton, 1915), 7.

is otherwise presented as an uncoupling of his "manly" self-regard. For Pienaar, self-sacrifice represents a route to wholeness, a rejoining of himself with God that will release him from his suffering and give back to him the spirit of masculine strength lost in dismemberment: "Peter, I could see, had the notion that his time here wouldn't be very long, and he liked to think that when he got his release he would find once more the old rapture" (*MS* 231). Conceived as both self-overcoming and a giving so that others might live on, Pienaar's self-sacrifice denotes a means of individual re-constitution consummated in death. Pienaar spurs Hannay into a manlier frame of mind, but his self-sacrifice is also quite clearly meant to represent a national re-invigoration in which a besieged Englishness is empowered by personal loss, for Pienaar's private struggles with Lensch indicate a confrontation between ace pilots as much as they signify the larger contest between nations: "there were plenty of fellows who saw the campaign as a struggle not between Hun and Briton but between Lensch and Pienaar" (*MS* 13). In death, Pienaar revitalizes both his own sense of identity *and* the identity of that which he defends, a vitiated nation brought back to full health through the necessary loss of one of its adopted sons.

Mr Standfast draws on a chivalric mythology of warfare—that "[g]reat courage," Wilfred Ward wrote in 1916, "the realization of a great and inspiring cause, [that] is equal to any trial that life may bring"—but equally it insists on the brutality of a war which would claim, in total, roughly forty million lives.[37] Buchan himself was not spared in this respect, losing a number of close friends, whom he commemorated in *These for Remembrance* (1919), and his youngest brother Alastair at the Battle of Arras in 1917, whom Buchan commemorated in a poem eventually published in 1936. That poem's image of a "ransomed world," by which Buchan means a world delivered from war at the cost of an entire generation, echoes right through *Mr Standfast*, most obviously in its depiction of traumatized male bodies.[38] *Greenmantle* glimpses at the nightmare of Front Line battle, but *Mr Standfast* puts bodily mutilation and disfigurement centre stage. Broken bodies and the threat of amputation loom large in this text, not least in the example of Pienaar, who refuses to allow radical surgery to be performed on his "wrecked" (*MS* 225) leg. Westwater, a soldier previously under Hannay's care, lies

---

[37] Wilfred Ward, "War and the Ideal of Chivalry," in *For the Right: Essays and Addresses by Members of the "Fight for Right Movement"* (London: Unwin, 1916), 32-52, at 34.

[38] "Alastair Buchan" (1917), in *John Buchan's Collected Poems*, eds Andrew Lownie and William Milne (Aberdeen: Scottish Cultural Press, 1996), 152-6, at 152.

waiting in hospital with a foot smashed by a shell: "'They say they'll have to cut it off'" (*MS* 296), he laments. Soldiers in the trenches are described as emaciated husks, shadows of their former selves: "'they looked like ghosts who had been years in muddy graves. White faces and dazed eyes and leaden feet'" (*MS* 172). And even shell-shock, that most insidious of disablements, is here represented bodily. Though ostensibly unhurt by a run-in with a shell-burst, Blaikie's psychosis is betrayed by his nerves and queasy inertia (*MS* 10-11).

These lesions, fractures, and bruises are the local signs of broader social and cultural ruptures. In later years Buchan would argue that World War One had been a global conflict that annihilated an entire generation and triggered a splintering of shared public values, a meltdown the likes of which, so he contended, had not been seen in centuries. In *Memory Hold-the-Door* Buchan states:

> The War, the vastest disordering since the breakdown of the Pax Romana, must be followed by decades of suffering and penury. Many familiar things had gone, and many more would go. Britain had lost for good her old security in the world, and, like other peoples, she would have to struggle to preserve stability at home. (*MHD* 180)

Clearly, then, the crippling effects of the Great War were still paramount in Buchan's thinking more than twenty years after it had come to a close, but he was no less alert to these concerns during the period in question. *Greenmantle* and *Mr Standfast* are, in different ways, diagnostic narratives that offer readings of cultural dissolution and decay just as they chart the effects of such decline upon individual human units. As Buchan's sister, Anna, put it, they are "a great deal more than mere thrillers."[39] The seriousness of these diagnoses ought to alert us as readers (and as critics) to their atypical status as contemporary readings of the tragedy of the Great War. We should perhaps see them as popular anticipations of those late-1920s "disenchanted" accounts of 1914-1918 as an unprecedentedly destructive moment in human history, texts such as Richard Aldington's *Death of a Hero* (1929), Eric Maria Remarque's *All Quiet on the Western Front* (1929), or Henry Williamson's *The Patriot's Progress* (1930).

---

[39] Anna Buchan, *Unforgettable, Unforgotten* (London: Hodder, 1945), 143.

CHAPTER FOUR

WAR'S SHADOW

Juanita Kruse rightly notes that "[j]ust before World War I Buchan had begun to think in broader terms of civilization rather than in the narrower concept of empire, but the war marked the watershed in his thought."[1] Empire, of course, remained fundamental to Buchan throughout his life and writings, but this local shift between "empire" and "civilization" turns on a particular conception of the War as an extended moment of breakdown. The Buchan Papers maintained at the National Library of Scotland include a text believed to have been written by Buchan in 1918 entitled "The British Military Achievement." In that document the author writes of the direct past: "Our perspective has suffered such violent changes and there is so great a gulf between the new age and the old that it requires some effort of the mind to realise what this means."[2] The imagery here, by Buchan or otherwise, presents the War as a potentially unfathomable, unbridgeable chasm between the now and what preceded it, a view of a break in the fabric of time that chimes with Buchan's description of the War in *These for Remembrance* (1919) as an irruption of primitive forces into history, an "elemental region of death and hazard and sacrifice where fortitude [was] tested in the ancient way."[3] Both readings converge in their account of the War as a break between one state of affairs and another, an image that would reappear in Buchan's later descriptions of the War as "the point of contact of a world vanishing and a world arriving" (*MHD* 166). Certainly, Buchan was constant in his belief that "past, present, and future are in a true sense indivisible, that we enter upon a heritage bequeathed by others, and that in our turn we hand on a potent legacy to those who follow after" (*HR* 151), but, in its

---

[1] Kruse, *John Buchan and the Idea of Empire*, 95.
[2] Buchan, "The British Military Achievement" [1918], Buchan Papers, National Library of Scotland, Acc. 11627, Box 40/2 ("Some First World War papers of JB"), unpaginated.
[3] Buchan, *These for Remembrance* (1919), introd. Peter Vansittart (London: Buchan & Enright, 1987), 13.

excessiveness and sheer sense of injustice, the War seemed to challenge such a philosophy.[4] Indeed, the Great War as sweeping "fissure" was a notion that gained much wider cultural currency in the years that followed, and across well-entrenched divides of politics and belief. For example, Wyndham Lewis, hardly a writer with whom Buchan had much in common, wrote in "The Children of the New Epoch" (1921) that the War was "like a mountain range that has suddenly risen as a barrier, which should be interpreted as an indication of our path. There is no passage back across that to the lands of yesterday."[5]

One of Buchan's preoccupations during the immediate post-war years (and the decade that followed) was to make sense of this "mountain range" and to document its effects on the societies still in its shade. Buchan's work from this period, like that of many others, was "post-war" not only in the sense of "coming after 1918," but also in the sense of having been *formed* through the events of the First World War. Even a work as seemingly unconcerned with its contemporary moment as *The Path of the King* (1921) shows signs of this second sense of the term, with its resonant allusions to those generations of sons and daughters who "blunder and sin and perish," while "the race goes on, for there is a fierce stuff of life in it."[6] But Buchan's stock-taking began in earnest in pieces such as "The Great Captains," an essay published in *Homilies and Recreations* (1926) but originally addressed to the Edinburgh Philosophical Institution in 1920. Buchan opens: "To-day we are very weary of war, and there is no one of us but hopes that in the future, by some happy conversion of heart and an adjustment of the mechanism of Government, the danger of it may be lessened and may ultimately disappear from the world" (*HR* 67). Buchan directly qualified this view in saying that "our interest in war will not cease with its abolition. Even if that interest be only historical it must continue, for since the beginning of recorded time war has been the

---

[4] Buchan did come to see the War as part of a set of particular historical trajectories. This resulted in some interesting claims. For instance, Buchan argued that the First World War "may be said to have superseded, so far as military interest goes, the campaigns of the nineteenth and early twentieth centuries," but, for him, America's Civil War could not be said to have been superseded in this fashion, "for in that four years' struggle," Buchan contended, "all the main strategic and tactical developments of the Great War were foreshadowed. Its scale may have been small, but we must not confuse scale with kind, and its quality was transcendent" (*HR* 152-3).

[5] "The Children of the New Epoch" (1921), in *Wyndham Lewis on Art: Collected Writings, 1913-1956*, eds Walter Michel and C. J. Fox (New York: Funk & Wagnalls), 195-6, at 195.

[6] Buchan, *The Path of the King* (1921) (London: Nelson, 1923), 11.

preoccupation of the leaders of mankind, and we mortals must have a perpetual curiosity about all great human effort" (*HR* 67).

Contrast Buchan's emphasis here on "abolition" with the ideas he advanced in "Count Tolstoi and the Idealism of War" (1904). In that essay Buchan argued that war "can only be banished from the world by debasing human nature; for war implies seriousness, and if the human race is only made frivolous enough, the Saturnian era will no doubt begin" (*SEB* 299). Whereas in the earlier piece Buchan had denied the possibility of conflict ever leaving the realm of human experience, such a view, looked at from the far side of the Great War, was no longer tenable; the point, now, in the post-war epoch, was to *prevent* a repeat of the cataclysm of 1914-1918 through historical understanding. Disastrous though recent history had been, ignoring that history on the basis of its horrors was not an option. The War, Buchan contended, must be met head-on, interrogated, and explained: as he put it in *Memory Hold-the-Door*, the "study of [history] is the best guarantee against repeating it" (*MHD* 199). This historical concern resulted in the republication of the *Nelson's History* in 1922 (now in four, much-condensed volumes), which was prefaced by Buchan's aim "to write a clear narrative of one of the greatest epochs in history, showing not only the changing tides of battle, but the intricate political, economic, and social transformations which were involved in a strife not of armies but of peoples."[7] "Strife" is a significant choice of word here, as it turns on a subtle double meaning between "the action of striving together or contending in opposition" and the more antiquated sense of "trouble, toil, pain, distress" (*OED*). This war, then, was in Buchan's view not only a literal contest between peoples but a complex, psychological *erosion* of the spirits of its participant communities.

Buchan began to dramatize the effects of this erosion in *Huntingtower*. This, the first of three novels featuring Dickson McCunn, explores in some detail the interrelated issues of post-war inertia, disillusionment, and weariness. While in certain respects the novel is presented as a light-hearted romp—note McCunn's view of its climactic ending as "the last act of the play" (*H* 162)—this should not be allowed to drown out its serious engagements with the problems produced by a radically transformed social sphere. In contrast to McCunn's momentary awakening to "a changed world" after "unhesitating sleep" (*H* 19), the broader narrative of *Huntingtower* itself depicts a distorted social landscape upon which markings of contest and loss have been glaringly inscribed. Following a

---

[7] Buchan, *A History of the Great War* (1922) (Annapolis, MD: Nautical and Aviation Pub. Co. of America, 1980), i. unpaginated.

brief "Prologue" set in 1916, in which we are introduced to the fragile Scottish soldier Quentin Kennedy and the Romanov-inspired Princess Saskia, the novel proper begins in 1920 as Dickson McCunn, a plump, recently retired, middle-aged Scottish merchant, sets out on a long-overdue walking holiday. On his journey he meets an assortment of characters: John Heritage, a survivor of the First World War, paper-maker, and a poet who, among other things, functions as a parody of modernist "fashionability";[8] the Gorbals Die-Hards, "unauthorized Boy Scouts, who, without uniform or badge or any kind of paraphernalia, followed the banner of Sir Robert Baden-Powell" (*H* 17);[9] and the beautiful Saskia, who is being kept hostage in Huntingtower House by a crew of Bolsheviks trying to find the jewellery she managed to smuggle out of revolutionary Russia. McCunn is inevitably drawn into "some black business" (*H* 105) and quickly sets about putting wrongs aright even as he doubts his own abilities.[10] Come the end of the novel, the Bolsheviks' leader (Paul Abreskov) has died at sea, Saskia has located her true love (Alexander Nicholson), and McCunn, now a Ulyssean figure "come back to Ithaca" (*H* 209), returns to his wife with a surprising gift: an emerald necklace "bestowed upon Dickson [by Saskia] as a parting memento" (*H* 210).

Despite its light-hearted narrative, *Huntingtower* is a novel populated by characters very much still in the shadow of the mountain range of war. As Ann Stonehouse points out in a fine "Introduction" to her edition of the text, "the war and its after-effects touch everybody in the story" (*H* x). This comes across most obviously in those military figures who took part in the War itself. Kennedy, for example, stands as a metonym of both individual and national tiredness, his ghostliness indicative of a vitality replaced by a "thin face with lines of suffering round the mouth and eyes" (*H* 8), and his stupors the symptom of a broader, collective exhaustion that seems to affect even the very masonry of his surroundings. Haunted by

---

[8] In her notes to her edition of *Huntingtower*, Ann Stonehouse suggests that through John Heritage's poetry volume "*Whorls*" Buchan may have been poking fun "at an annual anthology of radical verse called *Wheels*, which was edited by Edith Sitwell and appeared from 1916 to 1921" (*H* 218, n. 25).

[9] Panek rightly notes that the world created in *Huntingtower* is exceptional among Buchan's novels in this respect: "*Huntingtower* could almost be one of the Chief Scout's yarns for Boy Scouts. This novel, though, deals with scouting for boys, while Buchan was very much absorbed with scouting for men" (*The Special Branch*, 54). Buchan discusses the Boy Scouts in detail in *CO* 131-50.

[10] Consider the following passage: "Above them hung the sheer cliffs of the Huntingtower cape, so sheer that a man below was completely hidden from any watcher on the top. Dickson's heart fell, for he did not profess to be a cragsman and had indeed a horror of precipitous places" (*H* 112).

images of his fallen comrades, Kennedy's surroundings begin to take on a deathly quality as he is reminded of the Front by music from elsewhere: "The jigging music of a two-step floated down the corridor. It made the young man's brow contract, for it brought to him a vision of dead faces in the gloom of a November dusk. He had once had a friend who used to whistle that air, and he had seen him die in the Hollebeke mud. There was some thing *macabre* in the tune. [...] He was surely morbid this evening, for there seemed something *macabre* about the house, the room, the dancing, all Russia" (*H* 8). Although her son "had been in France fighting, and had come safely through" (*H* 38), Mrs Morran refers to a certain Tam Robison, who was killed on the Mesopotamian Front (*H* 39). Archie Roylance's catalogue of comrades is really, as he also observes of himself, a catalogue of cripples: "'There's Sime, my butler. He was a Fusilier Jock and, as you saw, has lost an arm. Then McGuffog the keeper is a good man, but he's still got a Turkish bullet in his thigh. The chauffeur, Carfrae, was in the Yeomanry, and lost half a foot; and there's myself as lame as a duck'" (*H* 143). And even John Heritage, the Poet initially for whom McCunn has nothing but dislike, is suffering from a mental anguish directly produced by his extensive soldiering. After being asked by McCunn about his period of service, Heritage answers: "'Four blasted years,' was the savage reply. 'And I never want to hear the name of the beastly thing again'" (*H* 24).

Bolshevism is presented in this text as the political corollary to these material and psychological disfigurements. Russian revolutionary ferment had already given Buchan a fount of jeopardy with respect to Moxon Ivery's double-dealings in *Mr Standfast*.[11] In the original release of the *Nelson's History* Buchan examined the Bolsheviks in more detail, wherein he viewed their rise to power—in Buchan's eyes, a variety of proto-totalitarianism—as enabled by four key dynamics: the (patchy) support of "the Soviets of the towns"; the widespread Russian desire for an end to the War; a desire for the land reform policies of Alexander Kerensky, the second Prime Minister of the Russian Provisional Government in 1917; and the utopian attractions of Bolshevism itself, "the passion for change, for anything provided it was novel, the dream of a new world which could only come into being after the complete destruction of the old."[12] For

---

[11] Blenkiron states: "'It was Ivery that paid the Bolshevists to sedooce the Army, and the Bolshevists took his money for their own purpose, thinking they were playing a deep game, when all the time he was grinning like Satan, for they were playing his'" (*MS* 214).
[12] Buchan, *Nelson's History*, vol. 21, 168-9.

Buchan, Bolshevism was a compulsion of profound mess, one ruled by violence, propaganda, and lawlessness:

> Like a drunken man, [the Bolsheviks] could only keep erect while they moved swiftly, for if they went slowly they would fall. To enforce their mandates, they enlisted *condottieri* from the gutters, the Red Guards, in whose ranks every miscreant found good pay and a life of license, and who formed a bodyguard for the Government that ensured them a living. It was all mad and chaotic, but it was not purposeless. Lenin and Trotski [*sic*] sought to bring about a world-wide revolution; to annihilate everywhere the *bourgeoisie* and the intellectuals, and to establish a proletariat tyranny. Chaos was their object, the chaos and destruction of the normal state.[13]

A key failing of Bolshevism, as Buchan interpreted it, was its desire *simply to smash*: "It had not been organized under the inspiration of a formative creed, and there was no scheme in the heads of its makers to replace what they had destroyed."[14] Furthermore, the total reform of class hierarchies promised by Bolshevism's ideologues merely took one variety of millenarian tyranny and substituted it with a second: "The under-dog was to come to his own. Since the vast majority of the Russian people were under-dogs, this sudden mass-consciousness swept even wise men off their feet; and, though here and there a thinker entered a *caveat* against jerry-built millenniums, he found no hearers. The Bolsheviks did not invent the class war; they found it the incoherent creed of the nation, including the bulk of their nominal opponents."[15] While Buchan saw an adventurous strength of mind in the Bolsheviks' machinations, for him, finally, they were little more than despots under alternative colours to those who preceded them.[16]

---

[13] *Ibid.*, 169-70.

[14] *Ibid.*, 170.

[15] *Ibid.*, 171. See also *The Island of Sheep* (1919), in which Sir William sees Bolshevism as an effort to establish "'the tyranny of a class. It's the same thing as Prussianism, only its class is the proletariat'" (Cadmus and Harmonia, *The Island of Sheep*, 73).

[16] Buchan writes: "As pacifists, they brought not peace but a sword; as liberators, they would enslave all but a single class; as levellers, they sought to establish a reversed tyranny, a shabby oligarchy from the pavement. It was this obsession which mastered alike the cold fanaticism of Lenin, the mild utopianism of Tchicherin, and the more supple talents of Jewish adventurers like Trotski [*sic*] and Radek. They knew that their reign could not last, but they wished to break down as much as possible of the old world in the time permitted to them, and to kindle a fire from the *débris* which would send sparks to the four corners of the globe" (Buchan, *Nelson's History*, vol. 21, 173). See also *MHD* 187.

To Buchan, Bolshevism equated to a form of fanaticism, a radicalism which he scorned in no uncertain terms.[17] As he wrote in *Montrose and Leadership* (1930):

> At certain stages in the world's history, destruction, wholesale and single-hearted destruction, has been the one thing needful. In certain crises, where something evil has to be rooted out, moderation and toleration may be synonyms for moral apathy and spiritual sloth. Men cannot be led to a worthy purpose by one who has his flag firmly nailed to the fence. Yet—and this rule has no exception—the extremist will only be a constructive as well as a destructive force if his extremism is based upon reason, and not upon the surrender of reason—upon a clear facing of facts, and not upon their emotional simplification. We dare not underrate the power of fanaticism, even of the craziest kind. Its strength comes from its narrowness, since its spiritual force has been canalized and brought to a mighty head of water. It has done great things in history, but these things have been principally negative—necessary negations often, but still negations.[18]

The hostilities outlined here are inseparable from some of the recurrent fixations in Buchan's historical awareness: the linked issues of power, authority, and privilege; the devastations of revolutionary social reform; and the opposition between rationality and obsession, to name but a few. From these interests grew a number of writings on figures caught up in issues of sovereignty and jurisdiction, including two books about James Graham (*The Marquis of Montrose* (1913) and *Montrose* (1928)), a supporter of Charles I during the English Civil War and a commander of royalist troops in the Wars of the Three Kingdoms, and a biography of the British soldier and statesman Charles George Gordon, *Gordon at Khartoum* (1934).

Buchan's fascination with such imposing historical personalities culminated in the immense *Oliver Cromwell* (1934), which discusses the Protector's role in the Civil War in exhaustive detail. It is a huge work that seeks to comprehend and explain (not uncritically endorse or side with) the revolutionary politics of its subject, and while it clearly favours Cromwell as a "great" who speaks down from his moment in history to subsequent ages, the book is characterized by a resolutely dualistic approach. It argues for what Buchan saw as the essential two-sidedness of

---

[17] Buchan rejected the revolutionary impulses underpinning Bolshevism elsewhere in saying that "in this world we cannot wipe the slate clean and write a new gospel on a virgin surface" (*CO* 21). See also *CO* 177.

[18] Buchan, *Montrose and Leadership* (London: Humphrey Milford, 1930), 11.

Cromwell's character: a humanistic Puritanism that existed with a brutal military genius in an age of contradictory, distorted idealisms. As he wrote: "Paradox is in the fibre of Cromwell's character and career. [...] a devotee of law, he was forced to be often lawless; a civilian to the core, he had to maintain himself by the sword; with a passion to construct, his task was chiefly to destroy; the most scrupulous of men, he had to ride roughshod over his own scruples and those of others; the tenderest, he had continually to harden his heart; the most English of our greater figures, he spent his life in opposition to the majority of Englishmen; a realist, he was condemned to build that which could not last" (*OC* 20). For Buchan, the task in accurately recording Cromwell's life was not criticism but *understanding*, a mission "hardest of all with one who sets classification at defiance, and seems to unite in himself every contrary, who dominates his generation like some portent of nature, a mystery to his contemporaries and an enigma to his successors" (*OC* 19).

   That revolutionary ferment was in Buchan's wider thinking at this time is evident from his pessimistic account of the Russian Revolution in his hastily-written chronicle of the sovereignty of George V, *The King's Grace* (1934). This critique, largely preserved from the 1922 *Nelson's History*, depicts 1917 as a year in which the ancient and the traditional began to be questioned, and it reads the Russian Revolution as a hopelessly idealistic catastrophe for the Russian people, one entailing "temporary dictatorship, the dictatorship of the workers" (*KG* 95) which came not from "the burning inspiration of a new faith" but, rather, a small fraction of self-professedly "representative" autocrats who led their nation to "another type of serfdom" (*KG* 94).[19] *Huntingtower*, by contrast, depicts the Bolshevism of 1920 not so much as a problem in itself but as the cover for other forms of disruption. Saskia is the principle spokesperson for this point of view. For her, Bolshevism is a transitory phenomenon, "'a government of the sick and fevered, [which] cannot endure in health'" (*H* 141). The real issue, as she sees it, is the state of Russia itself, which, due to the passions unleashed by the Great War, has become the cradle of international corruption: "'It is not Bolshevism, the theory, you need fear, for that is a weak and dying thing. It is crime, which to-day finds its seat in my country, but is not only Russian. It has no fatherland. It is as old as human nature and as wide as the earth'" (*H* 142). Moments like this indicate *Huntingtower*'s continuation of the social diagnosis of *The Power-House*—there is even a restating of the old view that "'civilization

---

[19] Note that in *Oliver Cromwell* Buchan argues that his subject "had no dreams of an oligarchy dominated by himself, with a king as a sort of Doge of Venice" (*OC* 302).

anywhere is a very thin crust'" (*H* 116)—and its adherence to Leithen's jurisprudential ideology. But they also indicate a shift in Buchan's views from a rejection of a specific utopianism to an anxious judgment of a world being torn apart by criminality, even if that criminality, as here, can be overcome.[20] In a comparable spirit to Sapper's *The Black Gang* (1922), the Bolsheviks depicted in *Huntingtower* are less actual utopianists and more everyday hooligans whose true objective is loot, "'certain jewels of great price which were about to be turned into guns and armies'" (*H* 68).[21] Moreover, these felons (Dobson, Leon, Spittal, and Loudon) are easily defeated *underlings* in the service of a greater enemy: the "Unknown" who turns out to be Paul Abreskov. He is one of the Bolsheviks' "'chief brains'" (*H* 116), a degenerate with "a slight deformation between the shoulders" (*H* 203) who is after both the jewels and the affections of Princess Saskia. And even *his* threat, however troubling, is containable. Abreskov perishes at sea during a storm, and his menace is cancelled.

What matters a great deal in *Huntingtower* is the various views of Bolshevism put forward by its characters. Perspective, in other words, is at the heart of this text. Kennedy looks forward to the Russian Revolution as an impending calamity, "a dark curtain drawing down upon a splendid world" (*H* 8-9), but this view needs to be read alongside Saskia's perceptive insights into the nature of the conflicts unleashed by the Bolshevik uprising. Her views, in turn, should be contrasted with the understandable ignorance of the young Die-Hards, Dougal and Jaikie: the latter sings a song about the proletariat as a kind of war cry (*H* 195), while the former, having attended a Socialist Sunday School, merrily sings ditties about class-consciousness and the "boorjoyzee" without having a clue as to what those terms signify. When asked by Dickson what the word "bourgeosie" really means, Dougal says: "'I don't ken. Jaikie thought it was some kind of a draigon'" (*H* 132). McCunn himself offers a sensationalist

---

[20] Thus McCunn to Mrs Morran: "'We want your advice, mistress,' Dickson told her, and accordingly like a barrister with a client, she seated herself carefully in the big easy chair, found and adjusted her spectacles, and waited with hands folded on her lap to hear the business. Dickson narrated their pre-supper doings, and gave a sketch of Dougal's evidence. His exposition was cautious and colourless, and without conviction. He seemed to expect a robust incredulity in his hearer" (*H* 53-4). Note that Buchan remarks in "The Judicial Temperament" (1922) that "[t]hough it is fifteen years since I ceased to practise I find that I still read the law reports first in the morning paper, and that fragments of legal jargon still tend to adorn my dubious literary style" (*HR* 209). See also *MHD* 90.

[21] Buchan argued elsewhere that "[i]f the soldier fights only for lust or plunder, he will fight ill" (*SEB* 297).

reading of Bolshevism that is noticeably rooted not in fact but in anecdotal legend: "They would carry him off in the ship and settle with him at their leisure. No swift merciful death for him. He had read dreadful tales of the Bolsheviks' skill in torture, and now they all came back to him—stories of Chinese mercenaries, and men buried alive, and death by agonizing inches" (*H* 152). John Heritage, who is viewed both by himself and by McCunn as a quite natural Bolshevik, contends that "'they've got hold of the right end of the stick. They seek truth and reality'" (*H* 28). What comes out from so wide a variety of accounts is an acute sense of difference: *Huntingtower* presents a society both plagued by the effects of Bolshevism and implicitly engaged in a communal debate over what Bolshevism meant to those who were living through its turbulences.

Class antagonism, of course, played a defining role in the Russian Revolution, and the schisms its quarrels engendered lasted well into 1920s culture and beyond. Buchan's narrator-figure in *John Macnab* (1924) notes this kind of social rupture with abhorrence, asserting that "[it] is a melancholy fact which exponents of democracy must face that, while all men may be on a level in the eyes of the State, they will continue in fact to be preposterously unequal."[22] But *Huntingtower* is noticeable not for a portrayal of proletarian rebellion but for its sanctioning of the bourgeoisie as, to quote Nicholson, that which "'will endure when aristocracies crack and proletariats crumble'" (*H* 206). *Huntingtower* reads bourgeois forms of identity as a unifying force from which Russian culture could learn a great deal, a force typified by McCunn, who is depicted here as the middle-class individual *ne plus ultra*. As well as his defence of the bourgeoisie from John Heritage's idealized comprehension of the proletarian classes as yearning for "'truth and reality'" (*H* 28), in which McCunn defines the middle classes as those that do "'three-quarters of the world's work and keep the machine going and the working-man in a job'" (*H* 29), McCunn is provided with a set of accoutrements that clearly locate him in economic terms. Sufficiently well off to be "philanthropic" (*H* 17), he also has enough income for his wife to be pampered at a health spa, "the Neuk Hydropathic" (*H* 13); he has a maid, Tibby; and he has built up a small library, including books by "Defoe, Hakluyt, Hazlitt and the essayists, Boswell, some indifferent romances, and a shelf of spirited poetry" (*H* 14) consisting of Browning, Keats, Shelley, Scots verse, and Walton (*H* 15-16). A recently retired merchant who "received in payment cash, debentures and preference shares," McCunn is "comfortably off,

---

[22] Buchan, *John Macnab*, 224. See also Cadmus and Harmonia, *The Island of Sheep*, 33.

healthy, free from any particular cares in life, but free too from any particular duties" (*H* 12). He is untroubled but directionless, a circumstance that suggests Buchan's aim here is not to romanticize or simplistically put bourgeois life on a pedestal, but to insist that financial privilege is not the end- but a possible through-point on the pathway to a better form of living. Indeed, one of the central journeys McCunn undertakes in this text is that which brings him into a closer relationship with his wife, from whom he has felt alienated "since their child died" (*H* 13). By *Huntingtower*'s end, their intimacy has been re-established. Although Mrs McCunn kisses her husband as she had not done "since Janet's death" (*H* 210) only *after* she has received Saskia's jewels, it is surely important that McCunn freely gives away the Princess' necklet of emeralds, "any one of which is worth half the street" (*H* 210), out of an altruistic tenderness.

A traditionally "romantic" ending this may be, but that is specifically Buchan's point, for *Huntingtower* signals its generic status as a romance throughout. This takes a variety of forms, not least by means of the text's constant references to the word "romance" itself. Buchan employs elements borrowed from fairy tales—"a beautiful princess locked up in a tower, a lovelorn suitor who is a poet and who helps rescue her and a mysterious villain who is 'the devil incarnate'" (Lownie, *PC* 169)—and in McCunn's transformation into "another man than the complacent little fellow who set out a week ago on his travels" (*H* 208) there is a Launcelot Wake-esque suggestion of chivalric becoming.[23] But "romance," too, undergoes a becoming of sorts in this text, inasmuch as McCunn's relationship to, and interpretations of, that category endure transformations of their own. For instance, McCunn begins his holiday by conceiving of himself in unsuspectingly mock-heroic terms as "Jason, Ulysses, Eric the Red, Albuquerque, Cortez" (*H* 17). Buchan resists using free indirect discourse here to ironize McCunn still further, but it is carefully established elsewhere that McCunn's views as to the "romantic" nature of his journeying are informed by opinions that have been filtered through "Romance as he conceived it" (*H* 89), and that his notion of romance, in turn, derives from readings in that genre (*H* 74, 152). McCunn's experiences never quite correspond to the somewhat idealized expectations those readings have afforded him. "What had become of that innocent joviality he had dreamed of," the narrator notes of McCunn, "that happy morning pilgrimage of Spring enlivened by tags from the poets? His

---

[23] McCunn's character origins, as *Huntingtower*'s dedication suggests (*H* 3), lie in the romances of Walter Scott, particularly *Rob Roy* (1817).

goddess had played him false. Romance had put upon him too hard a trial" (*H* 55). As he observes of his romantic muse: "This was not the mild goddess he had sought, but an awful harpy who battened on the souls of men" (*H* 80). Indeed, these frustrations acquire something of the status of a *leitmotif* in this text, as McCunn's recurrent recognitions of his views as deeply misinformed bear out: "Dickson groaned. What had become of his dream of idylls, his gentle bookish romance? Vanished before a reality which smacked horribly of crude melodrama and possibly of sordid crime" (*H* 53).[24]

McCunn's panic at this change from "bookish romance" to "crude melodrama" continues the text's ironizing of his quixotic *hauteur*, but it also signals a response to the ostensibly surreal that Buchan had been addressing ever since he began to invest in the thriller form as an appropriately "modern" mode of writing, and especially since the Great War had made him rethink the thriller's mimetic provenance. Modernity, in the form of industrialized warfare, had shown Buchan that the accepted understanding of the relationship between romance and reality needed to be re-thought. Whereas it had been assumed, by some, that the realistic was opposed to the romantic, Buchan contended in *Greenmantle*'s dedicatory epistle to Caroline Grosvenor that romance, now, never more so than in the era of such mass carnage, needed to be seen as a potential component of realism.[25] Accordingly, *Huntingtower* gives a more complex reading of romance than the binarism of the romance-realism dyad permits. Buchan suggests that romance is not necessarily an abstract spectacle that occurs in some idealized realm, but can be, under certain conditions, part of everyday experience.[26] On that footing, he implies that traditional accounts of the romantic need to be rephrased. The point to make here is that Buchan suggests that romance can be thought of as faithful to reality since twentieth-century modernity had shown that reality could exemplify what early modernism—in such a text as, say, *Romance*

---

[24] By the time of *Castle Gay* McCunn has become more discerning: "He alone of men perceived the romance into which he had stumbled, and by perceiving created it" (*CG* 247). See also *CG* 273.

[25] The passage runs as follows: "Let no man or woman call [*Greenmantle*'s] events improbable. The war has driven that word from our vocabulary, and melodrama has become the prosiest realism" (*G* unpaginated). "Prester John" (1897) anticipates this theme: see *SS1* 103.

[26] While it takes him some time to come to grips with the implications of such a view, McCunn himself seems to begin to grasp this in considering that "[p]erhaps all romance in its hour of happening was rough and ugly like this, and only shone rosy in the retrospect" (*H* 53).

(1903), co-authored by Joseph Conrad and Ford Madox Ford—had already firmly questioned: high ideals, unbelievable gallantries and twists of fate, and the reassurances of closure.[27] Even so, something of Buchan's ambiguous attitude towards romance comes out in *Huntingtower*'s final scene, in which the affection between the McCunns is described as follows: "Romance, once more, thinks Dickson. That which has graced the slim throats of princesses in far-away Courts now adorns an elderly matron in a semi-detached villa; the jewels of the wild Nausicaa have fallen to the housewife Penelope" (*H* 210-11). While this passage seemingly preserves a satisfyingly tranquil romanticism, there is a hint of mockery in the sharp distance between the normality of the scene, which occurs in a semi-detached villa in a Glasgow suburb, and its comparison of the Grecian, regal, and damsel-esque with bourgeois matronliness, a cosseted womanhood that, despite McCunn's plausibly rose-tinted vision of his wife, falls somewhat short of the Spartan heredity of the majestic Penelope with whom she is compared. At the same time, perhaps the joke is on a particular kind of "modern" pessimism here, with Buchan insisting, through McCunn, that middle-class "ordinariness" may, in fact, aspire to greater things than certain modes of thought permit.

Buchan's representations of Huntingtower House strengthen this multi-sided reading of the romantic. Before he actually sees the mansion itself, McCunn pictures "an ancient keep by the sea, defended by converging rivers, which some old Comyn lord of Galloway had built to command the shore road, and from which he had sallied to hunt in his wild hills" (*H* 32). The reality is less impressive:

> The outline of the building was clearly silhouetted against the glowing west, but since they were looking at the east face the detail was all in shadow. But, dim as it was, the sight was enough to give Dickson the surprise of his life. He had expected something old and baronial. But this

---

[27] With regard to *Romance*, I am thinking of moments such as the following, in which the category of romance is subtly questioned: "Journeying in search of romance – and that, after all, is our business in this world – is much like trying to catch the horizon. It lies a little distance before us, and a little distance behind – about as far as the eye can carry. One discovers that one has passed through it just as one passed what is to-day our horizon. One looks back and says, 'Why, there it is.' One looks forward and says the same. It lies either in the old days when we used to, or in the new days when we shall. I look back upon those days of mine, and little things remain, come back to me, assume an atmosphere, take significance, go to the making of a *temps jadis*. Probably, when I look back upon what is the dull, arid waste of to-day, it will be much the same" (Joseph Conrad and F. M. Hueffer [Ford], *Romance* (1903) (London: Gresham, 1925), 62-3).

was new, raw and new, not twenty years built. Some madness had prompted its creator to set up a replica of a Tudor house in a countryside where the thing was unheard of. All the tricks were there—oriel windows, lozenged panes, high twisted chimney stacks; the very stone was red, as if to imitate the mellow brick of some ancient Kentish manor. It was new, but it was also decaying. The creepers had fallen from the walls, the pilasters on the terrace were tumbling down, lichen and moss were on the doorsteps. Shuttered, silent, abandoned, it stood like a harsh *memento mori* of human hopes. (*H* 44)

Huntingtower's brickwork is a rotten pastiche, an imitation that flaunts its own fraud and, in so doing, merely highlights its status as a mock-up of some prior authenticity. In contrast to McCunn's decision-making, suggestively likened earlier in the text to the building of "a sober well-masoned structure" (*H* 14), the ersatz antiquity of the house is abhorrently, cariously modern: "[McCunn] had pictured an old stone tower on a bright headland; he found instead this raw thing among trees. The decadence of the brand-new repels as something against nature, and this new thing was decadent" (*H* 44). In these descriptions the fairy-tale castle that McCunn's romantic reading leads him to expect is displaced by a false archaism that is as objectionable to him as the faddishness of Heritage's poetry, which McCunn cannot but see as reliant upon "metaphors mostly drawn from music-halls and haberdashers' shops" (*H* 26), on the imitative routines and banausic contracts of elsewhere.

Like the monumental houses of H. G. Wells' *Tono-Bungay* (1909), E. M. Forster's *Howards End* (1910), or even Buchan's own *The Free Fishers* (1934)—respectively, Bladesover, Howards End, and Overy Hall—the Huntingtower mansion stands as a complex, contradictory symbol both of tradition and continuity, and of radical change and unrest. On the one hand, the house signals a link to the distant past: "The old lords of Huntingtower had once quarrelled and revelled and plotted here, and now here [McCunn] was at the same game. Present and past joined hands over the gulf of years. The saga of Huntingtower was not ended" (*H* 114). A complement to these historical echoes is a stark reminder of the spectral nature of Huntingtower House itself, the very windows of which are described as "ghostly eyes" (*H* 170). The mansion stands as "a lonely shell" (*H* 114), a tomblike husk in which "[t]he walls creaked and muttered and little bits of plaster fluttered down" (*H* 120). In this regard, McCunn's self-analysis as an "embarrassed phantom" (*H* 85) echoes the effect of the house's phantasm upon those drawn into its intrigues. At an earlier point, McCunn notes that the effect of the mansion upon his state of mind has been malignant, filling him with "revolt and a nameless fear" and a "foolish childish panic which took all the colour and zest out of life" (*H* 46). Saskia's extended stay at the mansion is an imprisonment, of course, and so to a certain degree her gauntness is explained by persistent anxiety, but for McCunn her haggard state and Huntingtower House are inseparable: "He saw the face of the girl in the shuttered House, so fair and young and yet so haggard" (*H* 86). However, we cannot ignore Huntingtower's essentially counterfeit nature, a radically modern identity (which is not post-war, as such, given that the reconstructed house, as the passage quoted above indicates, is twenty years old) that makes these responses to its ghostliness both reactions to aesthetic fakery and reflections on its history. Perhaps there is a hint here of the mansion as a marker of the *irrecoverability* of a history or tradition now lost to the present, a "blocking" that reaffirms Buchan's broader concern with the war as a midway point between two epochs, the former of which *Huntingtower* shows as disconnected from the present in the same way that the literal blank between the novel's 1916-set "Prologue" and its 1920-set opening chapter evokes the historical separateness of those periods.

John Heritage (about whom more in my next chapter) is of interest here, since at first he seems to denote an aestheticist practice in which tradition is ditched in favour of novelty for novelty's sake. Indeed, Heritage stands in stark contrast to the Huntingtower estate's antiquity, which has taken in, as Mrs Morran observes, "'great folk sin' the time o' Robert Bruce'" (*H* 40), while the echoes between the house's pseudo-nature and Heritage's modernist poetry arguably is part of a broader critique of the Ezra Pound-inspired cult of the new. McCunn himself offers this view: "He had a great respect for youth, but a line must be drawn somewhere. '[Heritage is] a child,' he decided, 'and not like to grow up. The way he's besotted on everything daftlike, if it's only *new*'" (*H* 30). And yet, despite these critical moves, Heritage is not an "easy" target in this text, since, like Launcelot Wake in *Mr Standfast*, he is clearly marked out as, and praised for being, an intellectual who has done his part as far as military matters are concerned. Although McCunn at first "could scarcely fit [Heritage] into even his haziest picture of war" (*H* 23), after learning of the latter's service in the Somme he is forced to rethink his notions: "Dickson had set him down as an artist or a newspaper correspondent, objects to him of lively interest. But now the classification must be reconsidered" (*H* 24). Heritage is one of Buchan's "half-antagonists," a figure who is, from a certain perspective, at first distasteful but finally shown "in a situation where he behaves as well as the hero, and proves that he too has the root of the matter in him" (Adam Smith, *JB*

260). If Heritage enters *Huntingtower* as something of a killjoy, he leaves it alive and well having played a vital role in the battle with the Bolsheviks that ends the novel. But Heritage's development in this sense remains separate from a particular kind of stasis apparently shared by Quentin Kennedy, and which *Huntingtower* hints at in the former's case but never confirms: that of shell shock. If Heritage is meant to bring to mind those few modernists who actually fought in the Great War, then he also carries with him the same, awful baggage. A noticeable allusion to Heritage as "demented" (*H* 46), which plays on a dual sense of "infatuated" and "insane," may leave the reader wondering whether or not Heritage's mental health is or is not cause for concern.

Indeed, although Heritage explains the title of his slim poetry volume *Whorls* as expressing what he sees as the sublime interconnectedness of reality, the narrator tellingly suggests that "whorling" might in fact represent "the most significant commentary on [Heritage's] state of mind" (*H* 167). And earlier in *Huntingtower*, when McCunn and the Poet first meet, it is precisely this, the psyche, that matters. To the former's view that "'there was something terrible nice about a wee cape with a village at the neck of it and a burn each side'" (*H* 33), Heritage asks: "'Ever read Freud?'" (*H* 33). Neither *Huntingtower*'s narrator nor McCunn, it turns out, has, and in what is perhaps the novel's most astonishing scene this lack of psychoanalytic reading becomes key. Shortly after locking away Saskia's jewels in the Strathclyde Bank, McCunn is besieged by doubts for which neither he nor the narrator can account. Whereas prior to this scene McCunn "found himself envying one whose troubles, whatever they might be, were not those of a divided mind," a division between "common sense and a desire to be loyal to some vague whimsical standard" (*H* 55), McCunn's mind now splits between a disgust at his own perceived lack of substance—"Suddenly the pretty veil of self-satisfaction was rent from top to bottom, and Dickson saw a figure of himself within, a smug leaden little figure which simpered and preened itself and was hollow as a rotten nut" (*H* 85)—and a vicious circle of choices in which whatever decision he might make leads to results he cannot bear. "The decision was coming nearer, the alternatives loomed up dark and inevitable. On one side was submission to ignominy, on the other a return to that place which he detested, and yet loathed himself for detesting" (*H* 86). While this scene is noteworthy for its keen imagery, these anguishes are left tantalizingly brief, with Buchan allowing his narrator to testify that "[t]he soul of Mr McCunn was being assailed by moral and metaphysical adversaries with which he had not been trained to deal. But suddenly it leapt from negatives to positives" (*H* 86).

Buchan greatly enlarged on the kind of psychological torment experienced by McCunn in the next Hannay thriller, *The Three Hostages*. In between writing this novel and completing *Huntingtower* Buchan's productivity had not abated. He wrote *A Book of Escapes and Hurried Journeys* (1922), which continued the romantic emphases of *Huntingtower*, and in 1923 he penned both *The Last Secrets*, an account of the some of the main achievements in geographical exploration between 1900 and 1920, and *Midwinter*, a historical romance. With Henry Newbolt he wrote *Days to Remember* (1922), a short, school history of the British Empire during the Great War. In 1923 he edited *A History of English Literature*, which covers the main periods of English Literature from Chaucer up to and including George Meredith, Thomas Hardy, R. L. Stevenson, George Gissing, Rudyard Kipling, J. M. Barrie, and Walter Pater.[28] Between 1923 and 1924 Buchan also edited, with Edward Gleichen, a twelve volume series entitled *The Nations of Today*, with individual volumes written by such noted contemporaries as Hilaire Belloc and the Oxford historian Robert Rait (Lownie, *PC* 190). Published the same year as Buchan's biography of the Earl of Minto, *Lord Minto: A Memoir* (1924) and his edition of Scots poetry, *The Northern Muse*, among other things *The Three Hostages* marks a continuation of the psychological analyses of *Huntingtower* even if it lacks some of that book's vitality and, indeed, the sparkle and briskness of the earlier Hannay books.[29]

The Three Hostages finds Hannay retired, so deep in peace as to worry about whether "it wasn't shirking to be so comfortable in a comfortless world" (*TH* 15), and married to Mary Lamington and father to the infant Peter John, named after Hannay's old friends Peter Pienaar and John S. Blenkiron. Now resident at Fosse Manor, the location of Hannay's bucolic rapture in *Mr Standfast*, his domestic bliss is ruined by the intrusion of Walter Bullivant, who brings news of three Establishment figures—"'the daughter of the richest man in the world, the heir of our greatest dukedom, the only child of a national hero'" (*TH* 26), as the Scotland Yard Officer Macgillivray puts it—who have been taken hostage by a criminal cartel aiming to profit from "the misery of decent folks" (*TH* 24). While initially

---

[28] For a brief example of Buchan discussing the process of literary canonization, see *HR* 12.

[29] This is perhaps partially a matter of choice on Buchan's part, since in *The Three Hostages* Hannay compares his earlier, wilder self to his more deliberate mindset of the present: "Then, I remembered, I had been thrilling with anticipation, but now I was an older and much wiser man, and though I was sufficiently puzzled I could curb my restlessness with philosophy" (*TH* 80).

Hannay cannot help but think that "[a] hideous muddy wave from the outer world had come to disturb [his] little sheltered pool" (*TH* 21), in the end his paternal instincts, helped along by Mary's adamant faith in her husband's integrity, compel him to act. With the pathologist Tom Greenslade, Sandy Arbuthnot, Archie Roylance, and the agreeable German officer Gaudian (first seen in *Greenmantle*), Hannay enters a frenzied, semi-mythic world in which "terror and mystery" (*TH* 67) lurk behind the safest of Establishment doors. This time around, the enigmatic wrongdoer is Dominick Medina, a friend to those at the heart of Britain's administrative community who secretly works all the while to become their overlord, thus hoping to subjugate civilization from within its innermost circles. Like all first-rate Buchan villains, Medina employs hypnotism as his primary line of attack, a power that here stems from the ancient foundations of medieval alchemy and Asian mysticism. In the end, Medina's plans run aground due to Hannay's efforts, but not before a collection of adventures in spots as diverse as a suburban nightclub, Norway, and the Scottish highlands.

The text's interest in the psyche is signalled in its first chapter, "Dr Greenslade Theorizes," in which Greenslade, a local doctor and one of Hannay's newest friends, airs his views regarding the nature of post-war forms of psychosis. Greenslade's key point is that the Great War led to a "'stark craziness'" (*TH* 12), one that eventuated "'a dislocation of the mechanism of human reasoning, a general loosening of screws'" (*TH* 13), a muddying of the "'barriers between the conscious and the subconscious'" analogous to "'two separate tanks of fluid, where the containing wall has worn into holes, and one is percolating into the other'" (*TH* 14). In this view of things, Dickson McCunn's psychological predicament (a mind torn between conscious choice and primal desire) is projected onto a general account of society: now, in the post-war era, the collective madness of the First World War has produced widespread individual lunacies. To Greenslade, consciousness and subconsciousness are no longer carved up into discrete entities in the average person, a predicament generative of a range of psychoses. Some such illnesses, as Greenslade points out, are more or less benign: "'With most people it's rather a pleasant kink—they're less settled in their grooves, and they see the comic side of things quicker, and are readier for adventure'" (*TH* 12). Others, meanwhile, are far less sympathetic. "'[W]ith some it's *pukka* madness, and that means crime'" (*TH* 12). To Greenslade's way of thinking this general wash of mental imbalance is of a more pressing urgency than shell shock, even, since for him the soldier's malady is but a metonym of a more vital shift in the psychological mechanisms of civilization at large. "'I say that you can't any longer take the clear psychology of most civilized human beings for granted. Something is welling up from primeval deeps to muddy it'" (*TH* 14). To Hannay's retort that civilization has been overdone and a little barbarism may bring back a simpler world, Greenslade can only sceptically reply:

> 'The civilized is far simpler than the primeval. All history has been an effort to make definitions, clear rules of thought, clear rules of conduct, solid sanctions, by which we can conduct our life. These are the work of the conscious self. The subconscious is an elementary and lawless thing. If it intrudes on life two results must follow. There will be a weakening of the power of reasoning, which, after all, is the thing that brings men nearest to the Almighty. And there will be a failure of nerve.' (*TH* 15)

The Three Hostages depicts this fusion of the rational and the primal both as a predicament of which to take advantage and as an injurious collective disorder. The former is evident in both Hannay's and Greenslade's mining of their own unconscious selves as a means of deciphering the poem dispatched by Medina to enigmatically publicize his Machiavellian scheme: Hannay is inspired to knowledge during a state of being "not fully awake" (*TH* 35), and Greenslade sets the pair's investigations up a notch by using exercise in order to push his "'mind into apathy'" (*TH* 41), leading to the discovery of a momentous clue (his prior, half-forgotten acquaintance with Medina) suppressed by his subconscious (*TH* 43). The world's madness, on the other hand, has produced a moral imbecility, as Macgillivray puts it, by means of which "a hideous, untameable breed had been engendered" (*TH* 23), a criminal nature not inhibited by the arbitrary barriers of nation, gender, or class. Whereas a safely "different" Russia may once have been "'a nursery of crime'" (*H* 141), now humankind at large faces a wickedness unchecked by traditional quarantine lines. If, as Arbuthnot puts it, "'[t]he old English way was to regard all foreigners as slightly childish and rather idiotic, and ourselves as the only grown-ups in a kindergarten world,'" the new, post-war world comprises a Balkanized humanity marked by unexpected antagonisms and aggressive rivalries in which even the forces of decency themselves are involved: "'[n]ow we have got into the nursery ourselves and are bear-fighting on the floor. We take violent sides, and make pets, and of course if you are -*phil* [*sic*] something or other you have got to be -*phobe* something else. It is all wrong'" (*TH* 63). Looming chaos, in short. Worse still, within this dilemma a hierarchy obtains in which "certain smug *entrepreneurs*" (*TH* 24) softly ply the strings of lesser malefactors quite unaware of their peonage: "the spectacle of these feverish cranks toiling to create a new heaven and a new earth and thinking themselves the leaders of mankind, when they were dancing like puppets at the will of a few scoundrels engaged in the most ancient of pursuits, was an irony to make the gods laugh" (*TH* 49). By contrast, the hooligans of Buchan's earlier narratives look slipshod.

In this respect *The Three Hostages* confirms and deepens what remains largely unexplored in *Huntingtower*; namely, that Bolshevism, problematic though it has been, indicates only the smokescreen of a deeper, more ancient kind of lawlessness, a prospect raised by Medina to a disbelieving Hannay: "[Medina] declared that behind all the world's creeds, Christianity, Buddhism, Islam, and the rest, lay an ancient devil-worship and that it was raising its head again. Bolshevism, he said, was a form of it, and he attributed the success of Bolshevism in Asia to a revival of what he called Shamanism—I think that was the word. By his way of it the War had cracked the veneer everywhere and the real stuff was showing through. He rejoiced in the prospect, because the old faiths were not ethical codes but mysteries of the spirit, and they gave a chance for men who had found the ancient magic" (*TH* 232).[30] Medina's primordial wizardry, derived in part from "'a manual of the arts of spiritual control'" (*TH* 134) composed by the legendary Scottish alchemist-sorcerer Michael Scott, is a particularly threatening combination of psychological and spiritual techniques that represents an expertise more ancient and advanced than that of psychoanalysis, one lying beyond the parameters of, and thus unintelligible to, those informed by its theoretical assumptions and professional vocabularies. Indeed, as with the threats of Einem and Stumm, one clue as to the true danger of Medina's skills is specifically the extent to which they must be limited by being explained away through the discourse of science to which they are rhetorically opposed. An early reference to Medina by Hannay as "[s]luicing out malice about my country, no doubt, or planning the ruin of our civilization for the sake of a neurotic dream" (*TH* 112) is given a telling boost in Hannay's claim that Medina's head-shape—"as round as a football" (*TH* 111)—suggests a degeneracy not unlike those specimens found in the criminal typologies of Cesare Lombroso and Max Nordau. But even the force of *that* description is finally displaced by the sheer iniquity of Medina's schemes. As Hannay reports: "His consuming egotism made life a bare cosmos in which his

---

[30] Buchan's interest in the narrative potential of "Eastern" occultism can be seen at a much earlier point in "A Lucid Interval," which explores the secrets of a "drug, capable of altering a man's whole temperament until the antidote was administered. It would turn a coward into a bravo, a miser into a spendthrift, a rake into a fakir" (*SS2* 122).

spirit scorched like a flame. I have met bad men in my day [...] but if I had had the trying of them I would have found bits of submerged decency and stunted remnants of good feeling. At any rate they were human, and their beastliness was a degeneration of humanity, not its flat opposite. Medina made an atmosphere which was like a cold bright air in which nothing can live. He was utterly and consumedly wicked" (*TH* 214).

A large part of Buchan's brilliance in *The Three Hostages* lies in making this figure of ancient evil, who "'exhales ease and power like a god [...] a god from a lost world'" (*TH* 192), directly relevant to the emerging post-war epoch by suggesting that Medina's hypnotic powers, if extended far enough, could form the basis of new forms of mass propaganda. In Buchan's world, as H. E. Taylor rightly points out, "[b]eliefs and truths no longer grew out of common experiences, but could now be projected on to society by a minority of skilled controllers. The technology of mass communication—newspapers, magazines, and film— could be used to compress knowledge and events into powerful beams of opinion, directed on to individuals with an authority that they were unable to resist."[31] Buchan had been a propagandist himself during the Great War, contributing to C. F. G. Masterman's War Propaganda Department at Wellington House along with such luminaries as Arthur Conan Doyle, Ford Madox Hueffer [Ford], G. K. Chesterton, John Galsworthy, H. G. Wells, and others. But whereas Buchan saw his own propaganda writings as "clean" works only intending to preserve national spirit, *The Three Hostages* opposes such a view to a persuasiveness that uses "'all the channels of modern publicity to poison and warp men's minds'" (*TH* 49).[32] The fear here, never quite consummated in the novel, is that the propagandists may themselves fall prey to their own *modus operandi*. Medina, who holds to the view that "'[t]he only power is knowledge'" (*TH* 119), never fully controls Hannay, whose "intractable bedrock of commonplaceness" (*TH* 71) enables him to resist Medina's conjurations, but he does initially attain to a level of power that is, for Buchan's hero at any rate, deeply disturbing. Like Sax Rohmer's Fu Manchu or Saruman in J. R. R. Tolkien's *The Two Towers* (1954), Medina's intonations strip others of their own speech-making and thought-processing capacities, transforming both the three hostages and Hannay into automata whose voices belong not to themselves. Sandy's reporting of such influence as

---

[31] H. E. Taylor, "John Buchan's *The Three Hostages*," *John Buchan Journal* 38 (Summer 2008), 48-50, at 49.

[32] Buchan later wrote that propaganda "can be a horrible thing when it means the dissemination of falsehood and bitterness. But it can be a very fine thing when it is directed towards a truer understanding by the nations of each other" (*CO* 81).

"'the most deadly weapon in the world'" (*TH* 65) only confirms what the reader already knows, that we are dealing with a profoundly altered and corruptible modernity, one in which psychology can be reduced to the status of an echo, and in which private language originates beyond the self nominally in charge of the speaking mouth.

In this way *The Three Hostages* anticipates and warns against the techniques of mass persuasion that would so characterize the period of Nazism and Soviet Communism, the time of a "million eyes, a million boots in line, | Without expression, waiting for a sign."[33] But if in certain respects Medina represents "'one vast lie'" (*TH* 87), as Sandy puts it, he also reveals unnerving truths about the plasticity of those in his company. Namely, a familiar Buchan theme this, the ease with which totemic assumptions may be turned against those already in their grasp: "He was just an ordinary good fellow of my own totem—just such another as Tom Greenslade" (*TH* 53), Hannay observes at first. Medina's presence as an "enemy within" is thus something of a comment on both the intramurality of perversion and the structures of complacency that enable such an infringement to take hold. Hannay's view that it was "sheer mania to believe that a gentleman and a sportsman could ever come within hailing distance of the hideous underworld which Macgillivray had revealed to me" (*TH* 74) is eventually revealed for the form of self-satisfaction it so obviously is. (Indeed, by this point in Hannay's career one would think, wrongly as it turns out, that he would be better at spotting evil-doers.) If Medina nauseates, insults, and endangers, he just as easily ingratiates and beguiles: "The poverty of the photograph could not conceal the extraordinary good looks of the man. He had the kind of head I fancy Byron had, and I seemed to discern, too, a fine, clean, athletic figure" (*TH* 44). And Medina's power, "a cooing voice and a shopkeeper's suavity" (*TH* 46), cuts across gender identities, attracting both men and women with equivalent disregard. To Mary he is "'extraordinarily attractive—no, not attractive—seductive, and he is as cold and hard as chilled steel'" (*TH* 192), while he fascinates Hannay "as a man is fascinated by a pretty woman" (*TH* 55) with eyes that "would have a made a plain-headed woman lovely, and in a man's face, which had not a touch of the feminine,

---

[33] W. H. Auden, "The Shield of Achilles" (1953), in Nina Kossman, ed., *Gods and Mortals: Modern Poems on Classical Myths* (Oxford: Oxford University Press, 2001), 230. Buchan wrote elsewhere: "I would rather have a young man talk the uttermost nonsense, provided it is his own, than repeat like a gramophone the sagacities of other people. He may be foolish, but it is better to be foolish than to be dead" (*CO* 160).

they were startling. Startling—I stick to that word—but also entrancing" (*TH* 52).

"Entrancing" is the key word here. *The Three Hostages* registers the changes in British society marked by the rise of mass democracy and the enfranchisement of women (*TH* 54), and it chronicles a distrustful modern world endangered by capitalist irresponsibility, industrial sabotage, political killings, and hostage-taking (*TH* 48-9). But it also signals a resistance to modernization in the form of urban development—"The house in Great Charles Street was one of those tremendously artistic new dwellings with which the intellectual plutocracy have adorned the Westminster slums" (*TH* 188)—and the emergence of the Bright Young Things, the unsettled socialites diagnosed in such detail by writers such as Evelyn Waugh, Aldous Huxley, and Henry Green. To Hannay's mind, certain sections of modern youth have fallen prey to a sense of liberation resulting in naïve abandon, one characterized by endless party-going and a susceptibility to what he sees as the harmful influence of jazz music. This is especially evident in Hannay's responses to the Marylebone club sought out by Roylance, who notes it as a place with "an evil reputation" where "licensing laws were not regarded" (*TH* 100). In Hannay's mind, the interior of the club—"a room with sham Chinese decorations, very garishly lit, with about twenty couples dancing, and about twenty more sitting drinking at little tables"—is a den of "rotten and funereal business," one where "[t]hin young men with rabbit heads and hair brushed straight back from their brows, who I suppose were professional dancing partners, held close to their breasts women of every shape and age, but all alike in having dead eyes and masks for faces, and the *macabre* procession moved like automata to the niggers' rhythm" (*TH* 101). As well as highlighting Buchan's occasional lapses into what we would now deem racism, this passage furthers the novel's reading of modernity in terms of the insensibilities it makes possible, finding in *les jeunes*, who include Medina among their number (*TH* 51), a liking for the "hideous ragtime" (*TH* 102) that turns them, in Hannay's view, into automata in the same way that Medina's victims become mindless slaves.

For so wild a story, *The Three Hostages* ends not with a bang but with a slow whimper. After freeing the hostages and thwarting Medina's plans, Hannay is content to have left his opponent powerless; "we had drawn his fangs, and for all I cared he might go on with his politics and dazzle the world with his gifts, provided he kept his hands out of crime" (*TH* 263). There is, however, one last battle to be fought. Medina tracks Hannay to his holiday spot in Scotland where he tries to kill him during a game of stag-hunting. Hannay catches on, avoids his enemy, and Medina perishes.

But it is the *manner* in which he dies that is important here. Hannay's reluctance to shoot even Moxon Ivery from behind in *Mr Standfast* (*MS* 194-5) demonstrated his Christian philosophy of fairness, even to an enemy, but it culminates in his unwillingness to let Medina fall to his death from a disintegrating cliff-face. Medina eventually falls, but Hannay is left wishing he had not: "Next second the strands had parted, and I fell back with a sound in my ears which I pray God I may never hear again—the sound of a body rebounding dully from crag to crag, and then a long soft rumbling of screes like a snowslip" (*TH* 295). This muted sense of accomplishment against an enemy now perceived as a fellow human being is anticipated in Hannay's earlier recognition of the drastic contingency of "progress" in the post-war world:

> I gathered from Macgillivray that though the syndicate was smashed to little bits he had failed to make the complete bag of malefactors that he had hoped. In England there were three big financial exposures followed by long sentences; in Paris there was a first-rate political scandal and a crop of convictions; a labour agitator and a copper magnate in the Middle West went to gaol for life, and there was the famous rounding-up of the murder gang in Turin. But Macgillivray and his colleagues, like me, had success rather than victory; indeed in this world I don't think you can get both at once—you must make your choice. (*TH* 263-4)

CHAPTER FIVE

HISTORY AND MODERNISM

Buchan's relationship to literary experiment is complex. In some ways he was quite clearly an innovator of sorts, one who pushed the thriller beyond the confines of the standards of Childers, William le Queux, and Oppenheim into one of its most recognizably modern configurations; he was a leading light who inspired entire generations of later writers and filmmakers to follow and build on his example (including, among many others, Eric Ambler, Ian Fleming, John le Carré, Ken Follett, Graham Greene, Alfred Hitchcock, and Valentine Williams). In Greene's words, "Buchan was the first to realize the enormous dramatic value of adventure in familiar surroundings happening to unadventurous men, members of Parliament and members of the Athenaeum, lawyers and barristers, business men and minor peers."[1] And yet, in other ways, Buchan was unashamedly traditional, locating many of his works within the established mode of historical romance as practised by his literary hero, Walter Scott, without essentially reconstituting the form that the latter famously consolidated. Buchan's historical romances provide wonderful recapitulations of and commentaries on the example of the *Waverley* sequence. Novels such as *Sir Quixote of the Moors*, *John Burnet of Barns*, *A Lost Lady of Old Years*, *Midwinter*, *Witch Wood*, and *The Blanket of the Dark* are works of imitation: admiring, creative imitation, for sure, but imitation nonetheless. As H. G. Wells maintained in his short review of *Sir Quixote* for the *Saturday Review*, "everybody begins with imitation," adding: "Mr Buchan has the essentials of a fine novelist—a picturesque imagination, a sense of close sequence, and some insight."[2]

But my account in the preceding paragraph is far from adequate. First of all, it reduces Buchan's historical writing to a blank uniformity

---

[1] Graham Greene, "The Last Buchan," in *Collected Essays* (London: Bodley Head, 1969), 223-5, at 223.

[2] H. G. Wells, "On Lang and Buchan," in Patrick Parrinder and Robert M. Philmus, eds, *H. G. Wells's Literary Criticism* (Brighton: Harvester Press, 1980), 83-7, at 86.

extending from his earliest work onwards. Second, it must be stressed that
Buchan's contributions to the genre of historical romance were not part of
some disavowed anxiety of influence, but a sincere intent to write within
the parameters of a literary mode that Buchan highly valued.[3] In "The
Most Difficult Form of Fiction" (1929), a short essay originally published
in *The Listener*, Buchan argued that the historical novel ought to be seen
as a mode of writing that, if appropriately attempted, made great, if not
impossible, demands on the fictionist. In contrast to those who saw the
historical novel as merely "a sword-and-cloak affair, a raw chronicle of
adventure," Buchan stated that "[a]n historical novel is simply a novel
which attempts to reconstruct the life, and recapture the atmosphere, of an
age other than that of the writer."[4] What should give us pause for thought
here is Buchan's apparently cavalier usage of the adverb "simply," for
how straightforward is it to enter into the spirit, and summon up the mood
of, the past in any believable, unadulterated sense? Is not all recollection
of the past inescapably coloured by present beliefs, thus consigning the
effort to capture history within narrative to a presentism in which today's
ideology is always-already part of the nostalgic view? Can the past be
known in the way Buchan suggests it can, so that a novelist who attempts
to record the activities of an age other than that in which he himself is
writing can represent the past as it really happened, rather than in the way
his situated opinions would retrospectively *create* that past, or is the
present not merely subsequent to, but entirely constitutive of, the ways in
which past events are identified and recovered?

Buchan was not indifferent to such questions, and this concern is
evident in his fiction; for example, in Janet Roylance's belief in *The
Courts of the Morning* that reality "'is what we make of things. We may
make them conform to our pictures. It is what we all do'" (*CM* 184).
Buchan recognized that the past was not purely "there" in some Platonic
realm untarnished by the beliefs and values of the historian construing it, a
view upheld by, for example, his idea of history in *Julius Caesar* as a
"palimpsest" (*MD* 94) of competing interpretations and his account of
"interpretative principles" in "The Causal and the Casual in History"

---

[3] The description of Clifford Savory in Buchan's *Sick Heart River* is in some ways
applicable to Buchan himself in this regard: "There were few men alive who were
his equals in classical scholarship, and he had published one or two novels,
delicate historical reconstructions, which were masterpieces in their way" (*SHR*
23).
[4] Buchan, "The Most Difficult Form of Fiction" (1929), *John Buchan Journal* 37
(Autumn 2007), 3-5, at 3.

(1929).[5] In that shrewdly-named essay, originally delivered in lecture form at Cambridge, Buchan states that "[e]very historian must have a thesis, some principle of illumination to guide him" (*MD* 5), making it clear that he saw the historian as a figure whose theoretical light, however dazzling, will inevitably shine on some areas and not on others, his prior assumptions (his thesis) deciding what will count as evidence for his history, and what will not, before that history is written. In opposition to those earlier figures who argued for a strong historical scientism (such as Henry Thomas Buckle, François Guizot, and Hippolyte Taine), Buchan contended that "[i]n the kaleidoscope of the past we cannot, as a rule, sort out effects and causes with any precision, nor can we weigh events in the meticulous scales which science demands" (*MD* 5-6). For Buchan, "disinterested intellectual curiosity" (*MD* 6) of the kind seen in some quarters as the historian's purview represented not some hopeless yearning for an uncorrupted, Archimedean form of detachment, but simply a pragmatic desire to do one's best with the materials and opportunities to hand, with "best" here meaning the vernacular mechanisms of good scholarship—thorough research, attention to detail, informed generalizations, and reasoned exegesis, among other things—loosened from "large mechanical principles of interpretation" (*MD* 18) based on abstract theories of human nature.

The meaning of "truth" was at the heart of Buchan's account.[6] Since, as he saw it, science is concerned with causation, with "proximate, or efficient, or final" (*MD* 6) principles, and since history is concerned with accident, "with broad effects and massed colours" (*MD* 6), Buchan argued that the objectives of each discipline, the "truth" aimed at by each branch of learning, must differ correspondingly. No slight against scientific objectivity was implied. Buchan's point was that scientific truth was out of place as a hermeneutic standard in a historic realm governed by chance. He conceded that the whimsies of history may unfurl in accord with some

---

[5] Buchan returned to this point in his biography of Emperor Augustus: "I am conscious that my interpretation of Augustus is a personal thing, coloured insensibly by my own beliefs" (*Augustus* (London: Hodder and Stoughton, 1937), 9). See also *MHD* 45.

[6] In "Truth and Accuracy" (1932)—Buchan Papers, National Library of Scotland, Acc. 11627, Box 31/4—Buchan discusses the relativism of truth and the provisionality of historical exactitude in detail. See also his comment in *Memory Hold-the-Door* that his early readings in philosophy afforded him with "a kind of relativism—a belief in degrees of truth and differing levels of reality—which made [him] judge systems by their historical influence and practical efficiency rather than by their logical perfections" (*MHD* 39).

"higher intelligence" (*MD* 8), but, since human beings have no unmediated access to the perspective from which such an intelligence could be mobilized, the historian who seeks to retrospectively explain human conduct must make do with an alternative standard of objectivity, a standard that ought to be finely differentiated from its scientific counterparts. "For history works under conditions wholly unlike those of the natural sciences," Buchan stated, "and historic truth must be something very different from mathematical truth, or even from biological truth" (*MD* 5).[7] That said, Buchan accepted that a certain kind of scientificity was required of historians, and he wrote that the historical Muse, Clio, "is a lady of many parts. She has her laboratory, no doubt, and her record office; she has, beyond question, her lyre and her singing robes" (*MD* 3). History, therefore, must be conceived neither simply as science nor simply as art, but as an interplay between the two, one in which history becomes "an art which is always trying to become more of a science" (*MD* 4) but does not aspire to the clinical perspective assumed by those faithful to "historical laws of universal validity," laws which look as if they provide "a clock-work uniformity of effects and causes" (*MD* 5). In Buchan's estimation, history was always a "movement towards" and not inevitably a "reaching," an "*attempt* to write in detail the story of a substantial fragment of the past, so that its life is re-created for us, its moods and forms of thought reconstructed, and its figures strongly represented against a background painted in authentic colours" (*HR* 95, my emphasis).[8]

Buchan's assertion that "[t]he aim of history is to tell the truth, so far as it can be ascertained, about the past life of humanity" (*HR* 103) did not always win him allies. Ezra Pound, writing about *Oliver Cromwell*, suggested that Buchan's historical practice equated to "a history for arm-chair retrospectors with a hobby," one that he contrasted with "a more eminent kind of history," most probably Pound's own account of tradition, "which would do its utmost to use past ascertainable fact as enlightenment to present, all too oppressive, problems."[9] For his part, Pound admired Buchan's novels, instructed him by correspondence course in C. H.

---

[7] Of "total" impartiality, Buchan wrote elsewhere: "Philosophically, it may have its justification, but I suggest that since fallible men must have their standards and stick to them, such detachment is rather for their Maker than for themselves" (*NFT* 11).

[8] As Andrew Lownie points out, Sir Arthur Conan Doyle deemed Buchan's short story "The Company of the Marjolaine" (1909), a narrative set in the eighteenth century, to be especially successful in this respect (*SS2* 98).

[9] Ezra Pound, *Selected Prose, 1909-1965*, ed. William Cookson (London: Faber, 1973), 266.

Douglas' Social Credit theory, and approved of his appointment as Canadian Governor-General (see Adam Smith, *JB* 292, 372, 382), but in this case he both underestimated and misread the subtlety of Buchan's way of thinking. It is true that Buchan's theory of history coupled an emphasis on veracity with an accenting of "pastness," in which the legitimacy of a given historical work largely was to be rated by its communication, however variously achieved, of the "textural" and "atmospheric" properties of a previous epoch. But this did not mean that Buchan saw history as irrelevant to matters of the present. One sign of this is Buchan's interest in what we would now call counterfactualism, a contentious branch of historical study that entertains "what if" scenarios (for example: What if Britain had never entered the First World War?) in order to shed light on the non-linearity of causation, and which Niall Ferguson defines as "a necessary antidote to determinism."[10] In this respect, Buchan's philosophy of history is one that combines an interest in the object of historical inquiry (the past) with a professional curiosity as to the nature of modern modes of historical explanation. Furthermore, and *contra* Pound, the frequency with which Buchan's histories allude to his contemporary world (both as innocent asides and as more careful comparisons) suggests that Buchan was anything but unmoved by the relevance of the past to the present. His point was that history should not be *subordinated* to present concerns in such a way as to make the chronicling of previous ages little more than a repackaging of "the now" in historical wrapping.

Buchan's view of the historical novel is inseparable from these issues, though whether or not he succeeded in marrying his theory of history with the requirements of fiction remains a moot point. In "The Most Difficult Form of Fiction" he noted that one of the genre's requirements was an "austere conscience," since "[i]t is fatally easy to project the mind of one's own age back into the past, and produce what is no more than a fancy-dress party," a form of projection he located in Tennyson's *Idylls of the King* (1856-85) and George Eliot's *Romola* (1862-3).[11] At the same time he claimed that too pedantic a historical method was similarly problematic, since the "danger of the historical novel is that it may acquire the antiquarian habit and reveal too much in the bric-à-brac of the past" given that a "man who has read himself into the heart of a past age may

---

[10] Niall Ferguson, "Virtual History: Towards a 'chaotic' theory of the past," in Niall Ferguson, ed., *Virtual History: Alternatives and Counterfactuals* (London: Papermac, 1998), 1-90, at 89. Also see Lownie, *PC* 179-80; *SS2* 2-3; and Macdonald, *CMF* 37.

[11] Buchan, "The Most Difficult Form of Fiction," 4.

come to value his discoveries for their own sake."[12] In practice, Buchan to some extent avoids what A. C. Ward in *Twentieth-Century Literature* (1946; first published in 1928) called "the nineteenth-century practice of attempting to suggest period-atmosphere by the use of archaisms," inasmuch as Buchan's historical novels, like those of Robert Graves and Naomi Mitchison, avoid outmoded expressions even as they take "the archaic" itself as the goal of their psychological representations.[13] They are, in other words, novels in which the attempt to render historically-relative forms of thought is prioritized over any fidelity to past forms of written or spoken language. The Lacanian objection that it is precisely language which enables historically particular forms of consciousness is not useful here, since Buchan's objective was not to reproduce historical "reality" as such, whatever that might involve, but to provide intelligible (that is, linguistically transparent) insights into the nature of previous epochs, insights that aimed for an appropriate sense of historicity even as they were inevitably limited by the linguistic confines of Buchan's "moment."

Witch Wood (1927) is of especial relevance in this context, as it is symbolic of Buchan's efforts "to discover the historical moment which best interpreted the *ethos* of a particular countryside" (*MHD* 196), and was to a large extent derived from the extensive historical study he undertook for his 1928 biography of Montrose (*MHD* 196-7). Indeed, Montrose appears in the novel as a source of psychological anguish and distraction for its protagonist, the young Presbyterian minister David Sempill, who is torn between his duty to the Scots Church and admiration for a man "who had been solemnly excommunicated by the very Kirk he was vowed to serve" (*WW* 81). A lengthy text, and Buchan's favourite among his own fictional works, the novel concerns Sempill's experiences in the Scottish parish of Woodilee near the ancient and shadowy Melanudrigull wood, which is revealed as both a haunt for natural innocence and beauty (in the guise of Katrine Yester's wanderings there), and for pagan ritual, devilry, and witchcraft (in the guise of his parishioners' involvement in Romanesque forms of worship). The novel takes place against the background of Montrose's Royalist campaigns during the years 1644 to 1646, and describes Sempill's growing distrust of his congregation, his fear and exploration of the gloomy wood, his passionate love for Katrine, the coming of bubonic plague, his scapegoating by Woodilee for the plague's arrival, Katrine's death, and finally Sempill's deposing and

---

[12] *Ibid.*, 5, 4.
[13] A. C. Ward, *Twentieth-Century Literature: 1901-1940*, 10th edn (London: Methuen, 1946), 55.

excommunication from his parish. There is a satisfying villain, the black magician Ephraim Caird, and the novel contains genuinely moving accounts of bereavement, such as the moment after Katrine's passing away, when the "world, the tangible world, was broken for [Sempill] in fragments" (*WW* 263), and a gruesome account of Bessie Todd's torture for being a witch (*WW* 211-12). Moreover, by means of his references to conspiracy and spying (e.g. *WW* 163, 217), Buchan makes it tempting to see the novel as not wholly distinct from the thrillers from which, in its historical setting and "neighbourhood" politics, it is ostensibly separated.

A fascinatingly didactic book, *Witch Wood* comprises an extensive range of Biblical allusions in such a way as to require heavy editorial annotation (for some modern readers, at least) if its often subtle references are to be followed. In Kate Macdonald's words: "It describes the religious controversies and civil strife of Scotland in the seventeenth century and is very deeply dyed in Reformation dogma" (Macdonald, *CMF* 195). *Witch Wood* certainly is a novel *about* religious experience, but it is also *built out of* religious textuality, and this adds to Buchan's efforts at realizing his narrative "historically," at depicting the mindset of a community during an era of intense religious debate and sacrifice. But history is approached in a number of ways in this text, one of the most interesting being that in which seventeenth-century modernity is shown to be functionally dependent on the archaic and primordial. As Sempill himself is addressed at one point: "'I judge that you are a ripe Latinist—maybe also a Grecian. You have read your Aristotle? You are familiar with the history of the ancient world, which illumines all later ages?'" (*WW* 45). Indeed, in this respect, to quote Cairns Craig, "[f]ar from being a historical novel, *Witch Wood* is an anti-historical novel, precisely to the extent that it perceives history to be the product of the continual eruption into the present of forces from the depths of the past in defiance of history's progressive development."[14] Likewise, Sempill is shown to be a man defined by his own history as much as the novel's historical reality is revealed to be a product of antiquity. A Greek scholar at university, "[w]hen religion called him it was as a challenge not to renounce but to perfect his past. [...] The beauty which was to be found in letters seemed in very truth a part of that profounder beauty which embraced all earth and Heaven in the revelation of God. He had not ceased to be the humanist in becoming the evangelist" (*WW* 20).

Witch Wood's frequent allusions to Sempill's "double" identity—for instance, that he has "the light-heartedness of a boy and the ease of a wise

---

[14] Cairns Craig, *The Modern Scottish Novel: Narrative and the National Imagination* (Edinburgh: Edinburgh University Press, 1999), 143.

philosopher" (*WW* 87)—feeds into a wider textual preoccupation with duality, a concern foregrounded at the text's outset by its insistence that in Woodilee "[s]ome held for the Devil, some for the Fairies—a proof that tradition spoke with two voices" (*WW* 6). It is clear from Sempill's interest in both classical writing and scripture, the half-Gaelic and half-Norse origins of the name "Melanudrigull," and, most obviously, the book's account of the conflict between paganism and Christianity, that the "dual" is a vital component of *Witch Wood*'s form. But *Witch Wood* is not a text that uncomplicatedly *upholds* duality, inasmuch as it is, say, a text that affirms binary oppositions. Not at all. Montrose's fleeting appearances in the narrative nonetheless reveal him to be a figure in whom binaries intermingle and unravel, a devil-man to some as he is a hero to others. Woodilee itself, characterized at the beginning of the text as a site of the holy and pure, is gradually revealed as a den of sin and transgression, an identity that obtains an objective correlative in the plague's decimation of the parish community, an outcome portrayed here as "an awful apprehension of divine wrath" (*WW* 239). One of the novel's most interesting characters, Andrew Shillinglaw, "something of a mystery both to parish and minister" (*WW* 107), points out to Sempill that even the most outwardly committed church-goer can inwardly be corrupt: "'It's the dacent body that sits and granes aneath the pu'pit, and the fosy professor that wags his pow and deplores the wickedness o' the land.—Yon's the true warlocks. There's saunts in Scotland, the Lord kens and I ken mysel', but there's some that hae the name o' saunts that wad make the Deil spew'" (*WW* 110).[15] And Buchan is careful to extend such a possibility to Shillinglaw himself by demonstrating that "there was always an undertone of satire in his speech" (*WW* 107), in this way setting Shillinglaw down as not an impartial commentator on events, however insightful his comments are, but an *involved* personage whose satiric viewpoint serves finally to highlight that he himself, like all the other community members, is capable of Falling.[16] That he does not is a testament to his goodness, but it strengthens and underlies Sempill's experience of his parish as a border zone between

---

[15] Thus Sempill: "The profession of religion was not the same thing as godliness, and he was coming to doubt whether the insistence upon minute conformities of outward conduct and the hair-splitting doctrines were not devices of Satan to entangle souls. The phrases of piety, unctuously delivered, made him shudder as at a blasphemy. The fact that his only supporter [Shillinglaw] was one looked askance at by strict professors confirmed his shrinking" (*WW* 111-12).

[16] I have in mind here the time-honoured view that the satirist's satire satirizes most of all he who does the satirizing. See Robert C. Elliott, *The Power of Satire: Magic, Ritual, Art* (Princeton, NJ: Princeton University Press, 1960).

good and evil, the "frontier-post for God's servant against the horrid mysteries of heathendom" (*WW* 22).

One of Buchan's stipulations as to narrative realism was a strong impression of "place," a requirement in part upheld by his career-long interest in the imaginative potential of sacred places (*temenos*). Katrine's mystical grove in *Witch Wood* is one such site, but the numinous copse in "The Grove of Ashtaroth" (1910)—a dualistic space, "ineffably gracious and beautiful, tantalising with a sense of some deep hidden loveliness" (*SS2* 156) that is yet home to a form of violent paganism—provides a more memorable, early example. For Buchan, the point of topography, and above all place-names, so he contended in "Literature and Topography" (1926), "is to produce an impression of reality, to link fancy to solid and nominate earth, and also to get from the use of sonorous names a certain verbal advantage" (*HR* 184). Buchan maintained that "[w]e live our lives under the twin categories of time and space; if movement is to be shown, one or other must be particularized, and since you cannot particularize time (for people do not have a map of an hour in their memories) it must be space" (*HR* 195). He stressed that "[a]ll concrete particulars, we are agreed, have their primary value in producing a sense of reality. The use of place-names on the grand scale gives an impression not only of the solid reality of the world of the poet, but of its spaciousness and its permanence. It produces upon the mind a sense of rest" (*HR* 195). This is not to say that Buchan underplayed the importance of time. His Preface to *A Book of Escapes and Hurried Journeys* makes it abundantly clear that in the *conflict* between space and time often lies some of the most intriguing possibilities for human endeavour. Buchan would place "time" in the ascendant, and in fine style, in his extraordinary novel *A Gap in the Curtain* (1932). This text draws on J. W. Dunne's *An Experiment with Time* (1927) in exploring the consequences of temporal foreknowledge, but Buchan was consistent in his view that "[t]he writer [...] who can build up in detail his background and dwell lovingly on its contours and its place-names, establishes an instant kinship, and is the more moving and persuasive because he appeals to a most ancient instinct in the heart of man" (*HR* 206). This approach informs *Witch Wood*'s strongly elaborated sense of space and place, especially in its beautiful descriptions of farm scenery, crop fields, and sunshine-strewn terrain (e.g. *WW* 18-19, 54, 69).[17] This is most clearly evident in the text's fantastic descriptions of the

---

[17] See also the scenery descriptions in "Afternoon" (1896), "The Herd of Standlan" (1896), and "Streams of Water in the South" (1896), especially at *SS1* 14-17, 57-8, and 76.

Melanudrigull wood itself, which shift between a Shakespearean sense of
an almost literal vitality (*WW* 87) and its menacing, deathly elderliness.

Just as Sempill conceives of Woodilee as a kind of frontier, so too does
he see the little glen in the forest where he meets Katrine as a "frontier
between darkness and light—on the one side the innocency of the world
which God had made, on the other the unclean haunts of devilry" (*WW*
97). Melanudrigull more generally embodies Reiverslaw's view that "[i]f
the Kirk confines human nature too strictly, it will break out in secret
ways, for men and women are born into a terrestrial world, though they
have hopes of Heaven" (*WW* 134). The wood, "the only opaque thing in a
translucent world" (*WW* 70), is the focal point of secrecy and hidden terror
in the novel, but it is also a foil for human values, most particularly
Sempill's, whose accounts of the wood and the community it borders shift
and switch as he becomes more familiar with its strangeness. Sempill's
early conception of Melanudrigull as lying "like a spider over the hillsides
and the mouths of the glens" (*WW* 33) in time gives way to his view of it
as a potentially paradisal site of "natural magic" (*WW* 87), and ultimately
as a natural space made foul by human activity: "The Wood had been a
nursery of evil, but might it not be purified and its sorceries annulled if it
were used for an honest purpose?" (*WW* 172). In this last respect, Sempill
comes to see that the wood itself is in some respects a vessel into which
Woodilee's parishioners, including Sempill himself, have emptied their
own prejudices and fears. This is evident when he helps the soldier Mark
Kerr into its limits in order to rest and heal: "Now the place was a shelter
for a friend, and a meeting-ground with one he loved, and the cloud which
had weighed on him since he first saw it from the Hill of Deer gave place
to clear sky. Men might frequent Melanudrigill for hideous purposes, but
the place itself was innocent, and he wondered with shame how he came
ever to think that honest wood and water and stone could have intrinsic
evil" (*WW* 176).

Compared to the contemporary works of such high modernists as
James Joyce, D. H. Lawrence, Dorothy Richardson, and Virginia Woolf,
Witch Wood stands as a very different kind of textuality. While it does
seemingly aspire to Buchan's totalizing definition of the novel as "a
representation of life in all its complexity, with a variety of characters and
a complexity of detail" (*CC* 210), "a solid and catholic presentation of the
whole truth [of life] through the medium of art" (*CC* 211), it is deliberately
and unapologetically backward-looking, eschewing narrative modes like
the stream-of-consciousness technique and the interior monologue in
favour of a particular kind of romantic writing much indebted to Walter
Scott and Robert Louis Stevenson. But this does not mean that Buchan

was indifferent to the varied practices of his modernist contemporaries. Buchan would later write: "During the War my general reading was confined to a few classics, but after 1918, feeling rejuvenated and enterprising, I did my best to get on terms with my contemporaries" (*MHD* 201). Moreover, he can be connected to many of the modernists through his numerous institutional, professional, and personal contacts. As Andrew Lownie explains, "with Vera Brittain, T. S. Eliot, E. M. Forster, Victor Gollancz and Bernard Shaw [Buchan] signed a letter protesting against the banning of Radclyffe Hall's lesbian novel *The Well of Loneliness*" (Lownie, *PC* 296). We have already seen that Buchan was on reasonably informal terms with Ezra Pound, and he was associated with D. H. Lawrence through Catherine Carswell (Adam Smith, *JB* 343), and Virginia Woolf through his wife Susan (Adam Smith, *JB* 161). Indeed, Woolf held an especial position in Buchan's view, and he praised her not so much for her fiction as for her acumen. As he recalled in his autobiography, "I thought Virginia Woolf, as a critic, the best since Matthew Arnold—wiser and juster, indeed, than Arnold" (*MHD* 202).

A loose sense of Buchan's attitude to literary modernism can be recovered from his own fictional writings. For instance, in *The Power-House* Tommy Deloraine describes Charles Pitt-Heron as "'perfectly capable of starting a revolution in Armenia or somewhere merely to see how it feels like to be a revolutionary. That's the damned thing about the artistic temperament'" (*PH* 5). Buchan would later criticize modern "revolutionary" fiction in the modernist vein for revolution-for-revolution's-sake, and he suggested that "generous youth, which begins with revolt, ends with acquiescence, simply because anarchy is not a creed in which a man can abide" (*HR* 62). Through its portrayal of the Jimsons at the Biggleswick garden city, *Mr Standfast* can read like an implicitly critical assessment of Lawrence's *The Rainbow* (1915), such as that moment when Ursula Jimson describes the Great War as "'a remote and secondary affair'" compared to "'the great fights of the world'" which are "'fought in the mind'" (*MS* 26). In Lawrence's text the similarly-named Ursula (Brangwen) portrays herself as an uninterested romantic who finds soldiers, and the wars they represent, insufferable.[18] That *Mr Standfast* tolerates pacifism but specifically rejects pacifist indifferentism makes this apparent allusion to Lawrence an unsympathetic one. Buchan was also particularly fault-finding of the Bloomsbury set, which harboured Woolf, Forster, and Lytton Strachey. In *The Three Hostages* Hannay observes that

---

[18] D. H. Lawrence, *The Rainbow* (1915), ed. John Worthen (London: Penguin, 1981), 357.

he "expected to be hidden by Medina to meet his necromancer in some
den in the East End or some Bloomsbury lodging-house" (*TH* 121), and in
The Courts of the Morning Sandy Arbuthnot is reported as saying that the
East "was simply dusty bric-à-brac, for the spirit had gone out of it, and
there were no mysteries left, only half-baked Orientalism. 'Go to
Samarkand, and you will get the chatter of Bloomsbury intellectuals. I
expect in Lhasa they are discussing Freud'" (*CM* 6).[19] While it is
necessary to negotiate between the voices of Buchan's narrators and the
voice of Buchan himself in these instances, modernism is sufficiently
scorned throughout his fiction to suggest that there is a kind of closeness
or affinity between Buchan's own views and those of his fictional
personae on this issue.

Huntingtower provides one of the most interesting of Buchan's
fictional modernists in the guise of John Heritage. We saw in my last
chapter that Heritage is the conduit for several themes, chief among them
the problems associated with various post-war psychological impediments,
but, as an aspiring poet whose verse expresses a kind of Sitwellian
modernism, he is also interesting inasmuch as his characterization
throughout the text tells us something about Buchan's attitude to the
aesthetic that Heritage represents. Heritage—whose very name expresses
an air of tradition opposed to his poetic practice—enters *Huntingtower* as
a writer whom McCunn cannot abide: "Dickson turned to other verses
which apparently enshrined the writer's memory of the trenches. They
were largely compounded of oaths, and rather horrible, lingering lovingly
over sights and smells which every one is aware of, but most people
contrive to forget. He did not like them. Finally he skimmed a poem about
a lady who turned into a bird. The evolution was described with intimate
anatomical details which scared the honest reader" (*H* 26). In contrast to
McCunn's liking for poetic daintiness, Heritage argues that "'[p]oetry's
everywhere, and the real thing is commoner among drabs and pot-houses
and rubbish-heaps than in your Sunday parlours'" (*H* 26). As Heritage
defines it,

> '[t]he poet's business is to distil it out of rottenness, and show that it is all
> one thing. [...] I wanted to call my book *Drains*, for drains are sheer poetry
> carrying off the excess and discards of human life to make the fields green
> and the corn ripen. But the publishers kicked. So I called it *Whorls*, to
> express my view of the exquisite involution of all things. Poetry is the
> fourth dimension of the soul.' (*H* 27)

---

[19] For a sampling of Buchan's critical remarks on the abstract qualities of Freudian
language, see *HR* 246-7.

What is interesting about Heritage's development as a character is that, in a crucial late scene in the novel, he himself "rejects" his own modernism by using his volume of poems for kindling. Alone and abominably cold, Heritage "regarded the book with intense disfavour, tore it in two, and used a handful of its fine deckle-edged leaves to get the fire going. They burned well, and presently the rest followed" (*H* 167). Given that Heritage burns his own artworks *without regret* tells us that the experimentalism they represent is "disposable," that it will not endure. And it is important that this occurs as a non-reported narrative event, for here the finger points not to McCunn but to Buchan: *Huntingtower*'s rejection of modernism (and Sitwellian modernism in particular) is, in the literal sense of the word, authorized.

However, to put the matter as one-sidedly as this is not sufficient, for in his literary-critical writings Buchan did offer a more careful response to modernism than the views one might draw from readings of his fiction alone. In "The Old and the New in Literature," a paper delivered to the Royal Literary Society in January 1925, Buchan portrays the tensions between conservative and radicalist (i.e. modernist) forms of literature as part of a long line of similar tensions throughout the history of writing, as a debate between those arguing for "the existence of eternal principles in art" and those in favour of "an atomic individualism and a petulant anarchy" (*HR* 43). The essay takes the format of two dialogues: first, between a lightly fictionalized Buchan and Theophilus, an "ecstatic admirer" (*HR* 46) of Proustian experimentalism, Bloomsbury, and Freud; and second, between this Buchan persona and Septimus, whose view of art emphasizes form and structure over "waywardness and slackness" (*HR* 54), dismisses modernism's anti-traditionalism as a lack of inspiration, rejects the accumulation of details in modern novels as a "photographic" but not "artistic" mode of aesthetics, abhors the sexual aspects of modernist writing, and blames the modern novel's supposed degeneracy on "'bright young Hebrews, male and female'" (*HR* 59). Read in conjunction, these two dialogues both shed light on the blind spots of the other and attempt to offer a more or less general account of modern literature as it stands at the time of Buchan's writing. Buchan sees the two dialogues as representing a clash of antinomies, "opposites but not necessarily contradictories," a war where one "may hope for an ultimate harmony and peace, but the victory of either side would be disastrous, for each is in the right" (*HR* 43).

This emphasis on the antinomial is key, since, as Buchan notes, behind the two debates lies "a surprising agreement. They recognized the same fundamentals, but from slightly different angles of vision. The full truth might lie in neither case, and both in their way might be right" (*HR* 60). Evasiveness is not Buchan's purpose here. Rather, "The Old and the New in Literature" validates both the views of Theophilus and Septimus in order to re-characterize them as context-dependent, the former being the avatar of adolescence, the latter that of wisdom: "As I reflected in my confused way, I wondered if there might not be two legitimate attitudes, the one proper for youth and the creative artist, and the other for maturity, the scholar and the critic?" (*HR* 60). And, again, characterization is important in this respect. Theophilus is "not one of those pallid, whiskered people in strange garments who live in aesthetic suburbs," nor is he a "product of black coffee and indifferent cigarettes" (*HR* 45). He is a youthful ex-army officer, rugby player, pipe smoker, a journalist, part-time novelist and poet, and, significantly, given that Buchan was persistently disapproving of socialism, "an earnest, if somewhat critical, member of the Independent Labour Party" (*HR* 46).[20] Septimus is a middle-aged gentleman, a distinguished classical scholar at Oxford, a revisionist historian, and possessed of "that stout conservative temper of mind which is found chiefly among those who in politics have been lifelong Liberals" (*HR* 53). The end result is a complex piece in which neither side of the argument is easily dismissed nor uncritically praised: Septimus is associated with a stale, unsophisticated Orientalism and Theophilus with an unproven cleverness, but Septimus is also praised for accurately identifying a "crude and partial" (*HR* 59) theory-hope in the young, while Theophilus' creed is seen as "clearly the outcome of reflection and not of natural bias" (*HR* 51). "As a matter of fact," Buchan notes, "the opposition is never complete; for the most fiery voluntary is not independent of tradition, and the most stubborn conservatism has its odd romantic moments" (*HR* 45). They are two sides of the same coin, separate but interdependent.[21]

One of Buchan's objections to modernist literature lay in what he saw as its origins in a kind of quasi-Paterian aestheticism. Buchan admired Pater a great deal, and wrote favourably about him in his contribution to the Oxford *College Histories* series—*Brasenose College* (1898)—as well as recalling in his autobiography that he had gone up to Brasenose itself largely on the strength of Pater's reputation as one of its Fellows. Although Pater died before Buchan sat for his scholarship, he wrote: "I

---

[20] A good sampling of Buchan's remarks on socialism can be found in Part Four of *Comments and Characters*. See *CC* 173-99.
[21] Thus Buchan: "I was beginning to think that Septimus was much of a piece with Theophilus, and that one whom I believed to be a *laudator temporis acti* was in reality an ultra-modern" (*HR* 55).

was glad to go to a college where he had lectured on Plato, and which was full of his friends" (*MHD* 47). Pater's influence upon the aestheticism from which modernism in part emerged, in Buchan's eyes, was an accidental one. It was largely a product, as he put it, of a set of strong misreadings. The aesthetes, Buchan argued, "made a fetish of style and a great parade of looking clearly and boldly at life, deriving their creed, I think, from a few misunderstood sentences of Walter Pater. In ethics they expounded an unscholarly paganism, they made little excursions in flamboyant naughtiness, and their style was a painful search for the inapposite word" (*HR* 63-4). For Buchan, a good proportion of this carried across into modernism, which he criticized in *The Novel and the Fairy Tale* (1931) for its lack of moral commentary; its highlighting of the crude, confused, and the ordinary; its fascination with the pathological; and, ultimately, its egoism and subjectivism (*NFT* 5, 6, 11).[22] Specifically writing about the modern novel, Buchan looked to such Victorian novelists as Scott, Dickens, Thackeray, Eliot, and Hardy as the out-and-out literary exemplars of the novelistic form. Buchan stood up for the view that

> [f]iction deals with ordinary life; but, without ever losing touch with the ground, it must somehow lift it into the skies. It must give it for us an air of novelty and strangeness and wonder, by showing beauty in unlikely places, courage where one would not have looked for it, the jewel in the pig's snout, the flower on the dunghill. A poet like Milton or Dante brings cosmic sublimities within hail of our common life; a great novelist makes our common life itself cosmic and sublime. (*NFT* 5)

Buchan's fivefold demand of the novel was that it tell a good story; that it judge its characters and their actions; that it judiciously select its narrative materials, rather than reproduce reality as "an inventory of details"; that the novelist remain occupied by narrative events, rather than his own responses to them; and that the novel itself be homiletic (*NFT* 7). Buchan's strategy for dealing with his contemporaries was to dismiss them as writing something *other*, something "based on a different theory of art, on a different conception of the novel," thus rendering their work legitimate but estranged: "These contemporary palimpsests of sensations and emotions and passions may have their scientific value, they have undoubtedly their literary value, but obviously they belong to an entirely

---

[22] Buchan also dismissed impressionism in painting as "too easy to be convincing, and when carried to any length it degrades the seriousness of the art" (*HR* 103).

different class from the books which we have been accustomed to call novels" (*NFT* 6, 4).

Buchan's account of the differences between modernist novels and that work which aspires to the "true form" of the Victorian novel is, of course, highly reductive, but Buchan was not alone either in tending to lump the modernists together as a single unit, or in underplaying the fact that experimental and traditional forms of literature in the period during which he was writing were extraordinarily intertwined and mutually defining.[23] Buchan's argument that the novel was only a novel if it hearkened back to its nineteenth-century predecessors relied on a monolithic conception of the novelistic tradition that left no room for tradition *as such* as a continual unfolding of new and disruptive forms. Put another way, Buchan probably would have wanted to take to task T. S. Eliot's argument that tradition "cannot mean standing still," even if Eliot's conservatism might have endeared him to Buchan's belief system.[24] This does not invalidate Buchan's line of reasoning, but it is worth citing as contemporary evidence of a certain kind of "perturbed" response to a modernism that has only in the past few decades been taken as a culturally heavyweight, rather than vacuously formalistic, mode of art. Besides, Buchan's critical account takes no notice of the fact that his own fictions—novels and otherwise—in places come close to, but always in the end shy away from, a formal experimentalism bordering on that engineered by the modernists who formed his critical targets.

Susan Jones rightly notes that "Buchan's first-person narrator in *The Thirty-Nine Steps* self-consciously plays with the kind of subjective modernist strategy employed by writers like Conrad and Ford."[25] The important point here, as we saw in my first chapter, is that Buchan engages with, but does not finally adopt through and through in this instance, self-reflexivity. Similarly, Buchan's view that "[t]he business of the novelist is to make men and women reveal themselves in speech and action, to play the showman as little as possible, to present the finished product, and not to print the jottings of his laboratory" goes against his own "trick of dissecting a character before a reader's eyes," which he cold-shoulders here as "abominably bad craftsmanship" (*NFT* 11). Such dissections

---

[23] For an excellent recent discussion of this mutual relationship see Robert Scholes, *Paradoxy of Modernism* (New Haven: Yale University Press, 2006).

[24] T. S. Eliot, *After Strange Gods: A Primer of Modern Heresy* (New York: Harcourt *et al*, 1934), 25.

[25] Susan Jones, "Into the Twentieth Century: Imperial Romance from Haggard to Buchan," in Corinne Saunders, ed., *A Companion to Romance: From Classical to Contemporary* (Oxford: Blackwell, 2004), 406-23, at 419.

provide some of the most crucial scenes in *Mr Standfast* and *Huntingtower*, for instance, with their psychological analyses of Wake and McCunn, respectively. Moreover, Buchan gave little explicit sense of how his fictions gradually approached a level of ambivalence that is, among other things, one of modernism's innermost staples. For instance, *The Thirty-Nine Steps* ends in the defeat of the Black Stone syndicate but also looming Armageddon, *Mr Standfast* with a fast-approaching end to the Great War but also the sacrifice of Peter Pienaar, and *The Path of the King* with Lincoln's death confirming him as "'the first American'" but also the double-sided culmination and end of the regal atavism, the path of the king, his life has signified.[26] And the split between hollow success and empty victory—in essence, a choice between parallel forms of lack—that ends *The Three Hostages* clearly exemplifies Buchan's interest in the un-decidable and the un-certifiable.[27]

The modernist with whom Buchan has most in common is Joseph Conrad. An admirer of Conrad's work, Buchan approved of *Nostromo* (1904), which he praised for its "subtle idiomatic knowledge," and, as Douglas Kerr explains, "as chief literary advisor to the publisher Nelson's, he was later to be responsible for issuing Conrad's *A Personal Record* and the Conrad-Hueffer collaboration *Romance* in a series of popular reprints."[28] Conrad, on the contrary, was largely antipathetic to Buchan's fiction, an antipathy stemming from Conrad's claim that Buchan's short story "The Far Islands" (1899) had plagiarized Kipling's "The Finest Story in the World" (1891).[29] These differences aside, it is clear that a good many of Buchan's fictions are post-Conradian in their makeup. As we saw in Chapter Two, *The Power-House* bears the hallmarks of *The Secret Agent*, but there is also a suggestion of *Under Western Eyes* (1911) in Lumley's view of Geneva as a haunt for "that form of foolishness which today we call nihilism or anarchy" and "crazy Russian *intellectuels*" (*PH* 31). Interestingly, given Conrad's early charge of plagiarism, in *The Thirty-Nine Steps* the literary innkeeper wants "'to see life, to travel the world, and write things like Kipling and Conrad'" (*TNS* 32). In *Mr Standfast* reference is made to a presumably fictitious article by Conrad in

---

[26] Buchan, *The Path of the King*, 344.

[27] Consider also the miserable ending to "At the Article of Death" (1897), which refuses the solace of religion in favour of a passing away "without hope or vision, with naught save an aimless resolution and a causeless bravery" (*SSI* 86).

[28] Quoted in Con Coroneos, *Space, Conrad, and Modernity* (Oxford: Oxford University Press, 2002), 70; Douglas Kerr, "Stealing *Victory*?: The Strange Case of Conrad and Buchan," *Conradiana* 40: 2 (Summer 2008), 147-63, at 152.

[29] For more on Conrad's charge see Kerr, "Stealing," 149-52.

the *Critic* magazine (*MS* 142), and the novel contains an ostensibly hostile glance at that article's author through Hannay's use of the alias "Conradi," which enables Hannay to pass himself off as a German spy (*MS* 247). As Kerr points out at length, Buchan's *The Island of Sheep* (1936) intertextually relates so closely to Conrad's *Victory* (1915) as to amount to a literary reconstruction of the latter text's ideological assumptions, with Buchan "serving the ghost of Joseph Conrad not with a theft, but with a gift."[30]

Kerr's reading of the relationship between Buchan and Conrad as one in which the former's writings provided closures and thematic transformations to the bleak and ambiguous fictions of the latter, described as a snatching of Conrad's literary method "from the jaws of its own defeatism," is also neatly captured, as Kerr explains, in *The Courts of the Morning* (1929), Buchan's tale of South American tyranny, revolution, and war.[31] There are numerous correspondences between the settings of these works: Conrad's San Tomé mine parallels the first of three mines—"the San Tomé, the Alhuema, and the Universum" (*CM* 64)—in *The Courts of the Morning*; *Nostromo* is set in the imaginary Republic of Costaguana, Buchan's in the fictional Republic of Olifa; and both tell the story of similarly-named mining towns, in Conrad's case, Sulaco, in Buchan's, Gran Seco. But even if a work like *The Courts of the Morning* hangs to a great extent in Conrad's shadow, there is still much to be said for its sociological reading of industrial modernity as involving a form of rationalization in which human individuals become faceless, regularized units.[32] The Gran Seco dictator Castor is the overseer of an army of drug-dependent initiates "'whose individuality seems to have been smoothed away, so that they conform to one pattern'" (*CM* 96), and Gran Seco city is referred to as a place of "extreme orderliness," "on one side a wilderness of furnaces and converters, with beyond them the compounds where the workmen are housed; on the other a modern city with high buildings and clanking electric trams" (*CM* 61). The city's smelting and refining plants

---

[30] *Ibid.*, 161.

[31] *Ibid.*, 158.

[32] Buchan wrote elsewhere that "[t]he Western Mind has a strong bias towards a reasonable individualism. It insists on regarding human beings as individuals as well as units of society. It always finds some difficulty in the mystic idealisation of the State as a thing with rights far transcending those of its citizens. In the last resort it regards the *person* as what matters. Therefore it insists on a high degree of personal freedom. It believes that we are men and women, and not animals living in a hive or an ant-hill" (*CO* 19).

(all run by the Conradian "Company") are places where, the reader is told, travellers

> [w]ill see the unskilled work done by Indians and mestizos—men with faces like mechanical automata—but the skilled foremen are all European. He will puzzle over these Europeans, for however wide his racial knowledge, he will find it hard to guess their nationality, since their occupation seems to have smoothed out all differences into one common type with a preoccupation so intense as to be almost furtive. (*CM* 62)[33]

This passage, with its Lawrentian overtones, is highly telling.[34] The "Indians and mestizos" referred to here are eventually liberated by the rebirth of Olifa itself as a free nation, but, significantly, the European centre their superintendents embody—what Don Alejandro describes as a bankrupt Europe being torn apart by Communism (*CM* 26), and what is elsewhere described as a place that induces "'bad effect[s]'" (*CM* 174)—receives no such renewal. Expatriates may be reborn, but Europe itself, it is strongly implied by the novel's conclusion, remains plagued by the forces of mechanization, passivity, and abjection—what the novel calls "distress" (*CM* 56), and which reappears in slightly modified form in *The Blanket of the Dark* (1931)—that formed such a central part of modernism's cultural diagnoses.[35]

The point to end this chapter on, then, is not that Buchan was a modernist nor that he was wholly opposed to modernist practice, but rather that his fictions seem to draw on the concerns of the modernism that his non-fictional polemics so clearly cross-examine. Buchan was angered but not confused by the literary pretensions of his youthful peers, and a careful reading of his *oeuvre* ought to give a sense of a writer who had thought about and exposed himself to modernism, even if he ultimately would

---

[33] The boss of the Universum mine is similarly motorized: "The manager was a newcomer who had been specially chosen by the Gobernador, a highly efficient machine whose pragmatic soul dwelt mainly in graphs and statistics" (*CM* 124).

[34] Compare this with Gudrun's response to the Beldover miners in Lawrence's *Women in Love* (1920): "Now she realised that this was the world of powerful, underworld men who spent most of their time in the darkness. In their voices she could hear the voluptuous resonance of darkness, the strong, dangerous underworld, mindless, inhuman. They sounded also like strange machines, heavy, oiled. The voluptuousness was like that of machinery, cold and iron" (*Women in Love* (1920), ed. David Bradshaw (Oxford: Oxford University Press, 1998), 119).

[35] For an interesting discussion of Buchan in relation to one of modernism's key anthropological touchstones (Sir James George Frazer) see Alison Milbank, *Dante and the Victorians* (Manchester: Manchester University Press, 1998), 218-19.

reject most of modernism's stylistic claims. He continued to write what he always had, a kind of literature characterized (wrongly, I think) by Ford as that in which the "values of life are apt to be very conventionally estimated."[36] Buchan was distressed by modernism, but that pain, I would suggest, was not something entirely inherent in the object itself (in modernism) but in the *way* Buchan opted to construct it as the other with which he fell into a kind of conflict. That said, Buchan can be seen to have revoked that conflict by entering into dialogue with his modernist contemporaries, sometimes implicitly but always sincerely. The best sign of this is "The Old and the New in Literature," which ends by allowing for the co-existence of both conservative and radical forms of literary practice. To suggest a Buchanesque modernism would be to mischaracterize Buchan's writing, but it is not pushing a point too far, I think, to consider that his fictions can be not all that distant from the modernism to which he would have them opposed. As we have seen thus far, and will continue to see in the chapter that follows, Buchan was certainly not a modern*ist*, but he and his fictions were certainly *modern*.

---

[36] Ford Madox Ford, *The March of Literature: From Confucius' Day to our Own* (Normal, IL: Illinois State University, 1994), 832.

CHAPTER SIX

THE PRESS, LIFE-WRITING, SPIRIT

Castle Gay (1930), the second of the Dickson McCunn books, is a novel about newspapers. Thomas Carlyle Craw, a mogul who, like Castor in *The Courts of the Morning*, lives a secret and protected life away from prying eyes. Having grown up from a precocious, Milton-reading child (*CG* 18) into a journalistic sage occupying "a roomy pulpit, from which every week he fulminated, argued, and sentimentalised with immense acceptation" (*CG* 21), Craw is a model example of self-determination, a figure who achieves success at the turn of the twentieth century with the *Centre-Forward*, a paper "in the vein of progressive thought, but also in the centre of the road, contemptuous alike of right-hand reaction and left-hand revolution" (*CG* 22). As editor, Craw steers his empire of print to a level of global influence, and the success of the *Centre-Forward* allows the creation of several more publications, among them *The Country-Dweller*, "a sumptuously produced monthly," "a children's halfpenny," "an unctuous and snobbish penny weekly," and "several trade journals" (*CG* 23). Craw's moderate imperialism leads to a new paper, *Mother England*, "a little slangy and vulgar, deliberately sensational, but eminently sound at heart" (*CG* 23). Eventually his articles get "printed in all his papers and syndicated in the American and Continental press" (*CG* 25). Described as "a thinker and an inspirer—a seer in a watchtower" (*CG* 84), it is said that Craw "had fulfilled the old ambition both of his parents and himself; he spoke from his pulpit *urbi et orbi*; he was a Moses to guide his people to the Promised land" (*CG* 26). He is a prophet among plain Britons, a man "who had taken upon himself the direction of the major problems of the globe" (*CG* 29).[1]

The price for Craw's success is his isolation, a retreat into a shell of privacy that is accompanied by "a molluscan dread of venturing outside it" (*CG* 27). Craw is agoraphobic, timid, and vulnerable to such an extent that

---

[1] Buchan's short story "'Divus' Johnston" (1913) contains the following view: "There was far more real power, someone argued, in the profession of prophet. Mass-persuasion was never such a force as today" (*SS3* 9).

his sensitiveness has become "a disease," while he guards "his seclusion with a vestal jealousy" (*CG* 28). Behind the veil of Craw's illustrious prophethood lies an alienated soul, "a self-satisfied, though scarcely a happy, man" (*CG* 27). His journey from this shy disadvantage to a figure of action, a "doer" (*CG* 132), discloses a textual commentary on the nature of a purely "intellectual" life insofar as rhetorical skill and cerebral facility are shown as but individual parts of a fuller conception of experience.[2] "'I thought him rather a dear,'" one character notes, "'but quite helpless. Talks just like a book, and doesn't appear to understand much of what you say to him. I suppose he is very clever, but he seems to want a lot of looking after'" (*CG* 64). Craw's cleverness (and, in a sense, his modernity) lies in recognizing that in his timidity resides personal failing as well as commercial promise: "He had the acumen to see that retirement was his chief asset; he was the prophet, speaking from within the shrine, a voice which would lose its awfulness if it were associated too closely with human lineaments" (*CG* 27). Thus Craw retires into solitude at the feudal "demesne" (*CG* 52) of Castle Gay, from where he rules his personal aides in a manner that is "arbitrary but not unkindly" (*CG* 28).

Like John Heritage in *Huntingtower* or Launcelot Wake in *Mr Standfast*, Craw is given "the root and branch treatment"; he is allowed to perform admirably in difficult circumstances (public speaking and international intrigue) in such a way as to transform him into a more endearing character. However, the world from which his success is drawn, the world of newspaper journalism, is subjected to a strong critique in this text. *The Courts of the Morning* is a key forerunner to *Castle Gay* in this respect. In the former text Buchan depicts the press as a significant aspect of modern policy-making, insinuating that political "reality" is to a large extent dependent on the way in which newspapers choose to represent it (*CM* 113-14). *Castle Gay* continues this emphasis. Craw's papers are viewed as "lying" in order to suppress conspiracy (*CG* 106), and reference is made to the fact that newspapers to a significant extent construct the very modernity they objectively claim to report (*CG* 245). This process of simulation, in turn, is reinforced by the suggestion that Craw's mogul personality has been little more than a "carefully constructed figure" (*CG* 200) paraded for consumption by a public whose opinions have already been formed in advance by sensationalist reportage. "'It is your newspapers that rule you,'" Craw is told by Count Casimir. "'What your man in the street reads in his newspapers he believes. What he believes he

---

[2] This is perhaps anticipated by McCunn's view "'that those who set out to lead the mob are apt to end by following'" (*CG* 14). See also *MS* 25.

will make your Parliament believe, and what your Parliament orders your Cabinet must do. Is it not so?'" (*CG* 109-10). Casimir's views are dismissed as exaggerations by other figures in the story, but *Castle Gay* seems to uphold his account of newspapers as both the formers of individual, mass, and even Government-level opinion through its un-named first-person narrator figure, whose views evidently match the Count's own (*CG* 151) as they are nowhere contradicted by events. *Castle Gay* presents the newspaper as a product of modernity that can lead to individual fortune (Craw) but also to a social levelling in which opinions are revealed as the end results of "'newspaper tricks'" (*CG* 61).[3]

Tabloids are the real target here, and in this sense *Castle Gay* continues and deepens Buchan's anxieties over the emergence of the so-called "new journalism" at the turn of the century, that mode of the Edwardian press "characterised by a bid for mass circulation—a bid aimed at the increasingly prosperous and literate lower classes—with news parcelled up into short and easily digestible portions, produced and sold using improvements in printing and distribution, and with advertising an essential part of newspaper finance."[4] During his time as editor for the *Scottish Review* Buchan argued that certain papers, such as the *Manchester Guardian* and the *Birmingham Post*, upheld "the old traditions," but he claimed that "by far the greater part of the newspaper-reading public prefers its penny print, where it can get its news, often inaccurate, in tabloid form, where it can be entertained with the less dignified kind of society chatter, and where the leading articles are, with one or two notable exceptions, the least important part of the paper" (*CC* 262). *Castle Gay* charts the development of this view. Public judgment in this text is in part condemned for being parasitic upon tabloid twaddle, a view put forward by McCunn: "He expanded on the modern lack of reverence for the things that mattered and the abject veneration for trash. He declared that the

---

[3] *Sick Heart River* presents the newspaper in even more critical terms. Looking down into the valley of the Clairefontaine river, Leithen is described as follows: "He remembered its loveliness when Chateau-Gaillard had been innocent of pulp mills and no more than a hamlet of painted houses and a white church. There had been a strip of green meadow-land by the waterside grazed by old-fashioned French cattle, and the stream had swept through it in deep pools and glittering shallows, while above it pine and birch had climbed in virgin magnificence to the crests. Now all the loveliness had been butchered to enable some shoddy newspaper to debauch the public soul" (*SHR* 41). See also *SHR* 152.

[4] George Boyce *et al*, eds, *Newspaper History from the Seventeenth Century to the Present Day* (London: Constable, 1978), 27. See also Patrick Collier, *Modernism on Fleet Street* (Aldershot: Ashgate, 2006), 1-37.

public mind had been over-lubricated, that discipline and logic were out of fashion, and that the prophets as a fraternity had taken to prophesying smooth things" (*CG* 157). For McCunn, tabloid journalism is to be criticized because it weakens the general standard of intellect in society and because it enables questionably manipulative propaganda to pass through daily life unregarded. Perhaps the most damning indictment aimed at newspaper culture in *Castle Gay* is the extent to which unfortunate human experience can be deformed and commercialized by journalism's lust for information, a charge it makes through the actions of the jittery Albert Tibbets, a reporter for Craw's rival paper *The Wire*. As Tibbets notes of Craw's disappearance early in the text: "'Don't you see we can crack the shell of mystery? We can make him *news*—like any shop-girl who runs away from home or city gent who loses his memory. We can upset his blasted dignity'" (*CG* 57-8). Here, private misfortune equates to circulation figures, with scant regard for the individual nightmares at hand (a point seemingly lost on Tibbets himself, who beforehand criticizes Craw for exactly the same brand of indifference).[5]

Craw's story plays out in the world established in *Huntingtower*. Two of the Gorbals Die-Hards (Jaikie and Dougal) return, as does Dickson McCunn, in a light-hearted story of international intrigue that is clearly indebted to Anthony Hope's *The Prisoner of Zenda* (1894). Hope's Ruritania becomes Buchan's Evallonia, an off-stage fictional European state which is used as the setting for the majority of the third McCunn novel, *The House of the Four Winds* (1935). A republic since the Treaty of Versailles in 1919, "apparently with the consent of its people" (*CG* 27), Evallonia is a country silently drifting towards Soviet Communism (*CG* 176) ruled by an ostensibly "'sober, stable, bourgeois government [...] always ready with the shibboleths of democracy'" which is in fact a cover for "'a camarilla of selfish adventurers'" trying to lead the people "'into the black ways of Russia'" (*CG* 206).[6] The entire story plays out against the backdrop of a local Scottish by-election, a surely allegorical move that

---

[5] Thus Tibbets: "'The *Wire* doesn't care a hoot for by-elections, but it cares a whole lot about Craw. He's our big rival, and we love him as much as a cat loves water. He's a go-getter, is Craw. There's a deep commercial purpose behind all his sanctimonious bilge, and he knows how to rake in the shekels'" (*CG* 56).

[6] In this sense *Castle Gay*, like many other of Buchan's fictions during the late 1920s and 30s, can be seen as a response to what he called "the modern craze for false doctrines—what the jargon of today calls 'ideologies,' creeds which seem to be accepted with a passionate devotion, as if they were new revelations, but which for the most part are the oldest of heresies, which were centuries ago exploded and discarded" (*CO* 50). See also *CO* 127.

implicitly weighs what *Castle Gay* presents as the fanatical intrigue of continental politics against the "open" mechanisms of democratic government. But the political aspects of *Castle Gay* are problematic because the narrative never quite takes full advantage of its opening premises. This is in part a symptom of *Castle Gay*'s comic mode, which threatens to trivialize the action being described, but it is also a question of coverage. The novel gets through a great deal of material, including returning to Buchan's interest in pacifism through the figure of David Antrobus (*CG* 181), but *Castle Gay* simply doesn't get on to a close-up account of world politics in the way Buchan achieved in *A Lodge in the Wilderness*, for instance, and we are reminded that the novel is an adventure story, rather than a work of strong political critique.

That said, *Castle Gay* can be seen as a small part of a larger engagement with the nature of authority that Buchan was undertaking during this period. At one point Craw is described as "a mild tyrant" (*CG* 28), a portrayal that feeds into the novel's broader concern with monarchist and republicanist antagonism on British soil, but also one that anticipates Buchan's *Julius Caesar* (1932).[7] In this text the Roman Emperor forms the subject of a wide-ranging biography that takes great pains to present Caesar as a Cromwellian figure (*MD* 56, 61) guided by a strong sense of pragmatism. Buchan contends that Caesar "was accustomed to look at facts in all their grimness" (*MD* 49), a man who "was above all things an opportunist and was content to let his policy be shaped by events" (*MD* 61). As Buchan represents him, Caesar was born into a hubristic Roman world marked by ideological façades concealing a decaying agglomerate of state mechanisms. Rome at the close of the second century BC was for Buchan outwardly a place of prosperity and "immense material progress" (*MD* 30) but inwardly of reaction, false imperialism, oligarchy, plutocracy, ethical decline, and administrative chaos in which "the whole machinery of the state was cracking under burdens for which it had not been designed" (*MD* 31). "It was plain to the wise that the affairs of Rome," Buchan writes, "for all her apparent splendour, were moving fast to a crisis, and the words spoken by Cicero half a century later were already being whispered in secret: 'No issue can be looked for from discords among the leading men except either universal ruin, or the rule of a conqueror, or a monarchy'" (*MD* 31). Buchan

---

[7] With respect to Craw's "tyranny," note Ford Madox Ford's contemporaneous view that "the most one-man concern" of the period was "the newspaper or the periodical publication," which he saw as "each of them of necessity more or less autocratically conducted" (*The English Novel: From the Earliest Days to the Death of Joseph Conrad* (1930) (Manchester: Carcanet Press, 1983), pp. 126-7).

distinguishes his account from hero-worshippers keen to present Caesar as having "conceived a plan of reconstruction" from the moment he entered the world of Roman politics, opting instead to focus on the behaviour of "a realistic intelligence" that "cast about him for the best methods" (*MD* 42) by which to proceed during a tumultuous period in European history.

Julius Caesar is in certain respects a study of competence, extending to Caesar qualities such as, among many others, a gift for leadership, a genius for incorporating topography into military strategy, a cool and precise intellect that remained so under pressure, and a profound sense of statesmanship (*MD* 75-6). However, Buchan was well aware that Caesar was a contentious historical figure who had grafted autocratic rule onto representative government. Citing Caesar as an example, Buchan argued in "Democracy and Devolution" (1908) that "[d]emocracy would be the most incompetent of all human institutions were it not for one trait which it possesses. It clears the way for the competent man, and when it once trusts it trusts whole-heartedly" (*CC* 12). Still, he admitted that this aspect of democracy paved the way for "too absolute power" (*CC* 12).[8] What is notable about *Julius Caesar* (which is by no means a sycophantic text) is that it attempts, like Buchan's biography of Cromwell, to comprehend, rather than unreflectively condemn, the psychology of a man facing hitherto unimaginable problems. Buchan's emphasis in *Julius Caesar* is laid firmly on the difficulties surrounding a historical subject plagued by global anarchy. Caesar "aimed at a civil commonwealth, but it was proof of the difficulties of the task that the word which best described the new sovereign was one associated with military command" (*MD* 95). As a dominative influence within Roman politics, Caesar was for Buchan a decentralizer and an encourager of Roman citizenship (*MD* 95), as well as a humanist "inspired by the two principles of the ultimate sovereignty of one man and of wide local liberties" (*MD* 96).[9] Whether or not Buchan was accurate in this portrayal, of course, is a wholly alternative question, but the reader is left with an impression of a figure whose world-vision had defects and yet which stood as a key inspiration towards subsequent generations of nation-builders: "Caesar had to make such bread as his indifferent grain permitted. Nevertheless, he offered his world a new evangel. For the first time in government prejudice was replaced by

---

[8] Buchan was aware of the dangers towards which democracy could lead, but he did not view the democratic impulse as a *necessary* precursor to authoritarianism: "Democracy and aristocracy can co-exist, for oligarchy is their common enemy" (*MHD* 66).

[9] On Caesar's humanism see also *MD* 97.

science and tradition by reason. He made the rule of law prevail, and gave the plain man a new order and a new hope" (*MD* 96).[10]

It is an intriguing quirk of history that Buchan should devote so much energy to analyzing Roman imperial authority prior to himself being awarded one of the British Empire's most prestigious official posts: the Governor-Generalship of Canada. During the early 1930s Buchan's life became even more hectic than usual. Towards the end of the previous decade he had become a Conservative Member of Parliament for the Scottish Universities; in 1929 he took on the role as an official adviser to the Conservative Prime Minister Stanley Baldwin; in 1931 he assumed a similar role for Ramsay MacDonald; in 1932 Buchan was considered for the Governor-Generalship of Burma; in 1933 he was appointed by George VI as Lord High Commissioner to the General Assembly of the Church of Scotland, a post he continued in during 1934 (Macdonald, *CMF* 30). Again, he undertook all these responsibilities while he continued to publish fictional and non-fictional works. Between 1930 and the year of his Canadian appointment, 1935, Buchan wrote six novels (*Castle Gay, The Blanket of the Dark, The Gap in the Curtain, A Prince of the Captivity, The Free Fishers*, and *The House of the Four Winds*), six biographical studies (*Lord Rosebery, Sir Walter Scott, Julius Caesar, Gordon at Khartoum, Oliver Cromwell, The King's Grace*), a children's story (*The Magic Walking-Stick*), plus two miscellaneous works (*The Kirk in Scotland* and *The Massacre of Glencoe*). In 1931 he edited a collection of the Scottish writer Neil Munro's poetry. The years of his office were no less productive. Between 1935 and 1940, the year of his death, Buchan wrote a further two novels (*The Island of Sheep*, which used the same title as his 1919 volume, and *Sick Heart River*), an eponymous biography of the Roman Emperor Augustus, an autobiography (*Memory Hold-the-Door*), and an unfinished story for Canadian youth (*The Long Traverse*).[11]

---

[10] Buchan wrote elsewhere that the "great Mediterranean tradition of Greece and Rome" was "the basis of civilisation" (*CO* 12), and he described the Romans as "the real makers of the world as we know it" (*CO* 196).

[11] Given Buchan's frenzied schedule at this point it is perhaps unsurprising that we should find Buchan writing in *Augustus* of the first Roman Emperor as an imperative precursor to modernity whose administrative competence should be closely scrutinized. Of Augustus Buchan writes: "History does not repeat itself except with variations, and it is idle to look for exact parallels, but we can trace a resemblance between the conditions of his time and those of to-day. ... In the actual business of administration there is no question of to-day which Augustus had not to face and answer" (*Augustus*, 345). See also *CO* 187-90.

Buchan's views on what a Governor-General should be and should do were clearly expressed in his biography of Lord Minto, who had himself been Governor-General of Canada between 1898 and 1904. In that book Buchan writes:

> A Governor-General lives an intricate and crowded life in the public eye, and he is fortunate if from the whirl of minor duties he can snatch time for study and reflection. His mind may be absorbed in some grave discussion with his Ministers or the home Government, but he must present himself smiling at a dozen functions, and let no one guess his preoccupation. He must perpetually entertain and be entertained: he must show interest in every form of public activity, from a charity bazaar to a university celebration; he must be accessible to all men that he may learn of them and they of him; he must visit every corner of his domain, and become, for the time being, not only one of its citizens, but by adoption a perfervid son of each town and province. These things are the imponderabilia of governorship, not less important than a cool head and a sound judgment in the greater matters of policy, and many a man who is well fitted for the latter duties fails signally in the other.[12]

Buchan was similarly torn between private reflection and public duty during his time in Canada but his official obligations included a number of welcome cultural tasks, which included contributing to the adjudicating panel of the 1937 regional arts festival held in Toronto. At this event both Buchan and Michel Saint-Denis reportedly suggested that "competing [theatre] groups ought to think more about ways to make audiences laugh in order to relieve the miseries of the Depression."[13] Although he enjoyed a prickly relationship with Mackenzie King, the Canadian Prime Minister, Buchan deferentially followed through his tenure, a deference at which he apparently grew more capable with time (Lownie *PC*, 252). While in Canada Buchan gave speeches on a variety of topics (collected in *Canadian Occasions*), among them public addresses on literary issues: "Return to Masterpieces," "The French Tongue," and "The Integrity of Thought," all of which were delivered in 1937.

Buchan can be seen dwelling on a number of "the greater matters of policy" in *Canadian Occasions*. Chief among them, perhaps, is the nature of democracy, a topic to which he would return in the most "literary" non-fictional book that he wrote during this final decade: *Memory Hold-the-*

---

[12] Buchan, *Lord Minto: A Memoir* (1924) (Teddington: Echo Library, 2006), 124.

[13] Denis Salter, "The Idea of a National Theatre," in Robert Lecker, ed., *Canadian Canons: Essays in Literary Value* (Toronto: University of Toronto Press, 1991), 71-90, at 88.

Door. Buchan discloses in "The Service of the State" (1936), for instance, that democracy necessitates "the whole nation concern[ing] itself with national questions and that thereby an informed public opinion is created which is the true sovereign" (*CO* 76).[14] Likewise in *Memory Hold-the-Door* Buchan expresses a conception of democracy much in tune with his earlier conceptualizations of empire, which he defined in "attitudinal" as opposed to policy-based terms. Writing of his time in Parliament during the late 1920s, Buchan recalls that "[d]emocracy—the essential thing as distinguished from this or that democratic government—was primarily an attitude of mind, a spiritual testament, and not an economic structure or a political machine" (*MHD* 220). Citing Hamilton and Jefferson as key antecedents, Buchan maintained this view in calling for a conception of democracy primarily marked by "a spiritual testament, from which certain political and economic orders naturally follow" (*MHD* 272). For Buchan, this "testament" had two principal features: that the ordinary man be given sufficient liberty to believe "in himself and in his ability, along with his fellows, to govern his country"; and an essentially Christian conviction "of the worth of every human soul—the worth, not the equality" (*MHD* 272). At the end of his life Buchan's view of democracy was thus a humanistic if not an egalitarian one, and it is in statements such as these that *Memory Hold-the-Door* stands as much more than autobiography. Buchan's view of America as "the supreme example of a federation in being, a federation which recognises the rights and individuality of the parts, but accepts the overriding interests of the whole" (*MHD* 273) would surely have resonated with its contemporary British and American readers, who were then faced with the prospect of a world being remade in accordance with the dictates of fascism.[15]

And yet if *Memory Hold-the-Door* is a text attuned to its historical moment, it also accentuates the continuing effects of prior histories upon that same present. This is explicit in Buchan's account of World War One. *A Prince of the Captivity* (1933) precedes Buchan's autobiography in this regard, but *Memory Hold-the-Door* is significant both for its mournful account of that "holocaust of youth" (*MHD* 256) and for its devotion of an

---

[14] In advance of this statement Buchan argues that the modern choice "is not between public and private life, for in a sense there is no more private life. An immense amount of government you must have; the alternatives are government which is confused and corrupt and government which is clean and competent" (*CO* 75).

[15] Given Buchan's fascination with Roman history, it is interesting that he deemed Mussolini's Italy to be a fanatical misinterpretation of Augustus' Rome (Lownie *PC*, 253).

entire chapter, "Inter Arma," to the conflict during the first months of the
Second World War, that time when "the mist [was] too thick to see far
down the road" (*MHD* 293). The Great War thus emerges as enduringly
significant in Buchan's way of thinking, a point made clear in the way that
conflict figures in the text's discussion of modernist experimentalism.
Indeed, *Memory Hold-the-Door* suggests that Buchan's account of
modernism is inseparable from his account of warfare. A particular
problem with post-War modernist literature, so Buchan argued, was its
reliance upon a subjectivist aesthetic in which erotic desire and the urges
of the subconscious were thrown to centre-stage. He praised Woolf for her
critical intelligence and delicate handing of Freud's theories in her novels,
but he insisted that "the mere digging out and heaping up of material from
the subconscious has no value" (*CO* 255). Buchan's culprits here are those
post-War writers who produced what he saw as shapeless, unruly fictions
by disproportionately accentuating the significance of the pre-rational and
the sexual as a means of explaining human behaviour. In a similar vein to
the critique of Joyce's *Ulysses* advanced by Wyndham Lewis in *Time and
Western Man* (1927), where Lewis admitted that novel's literary
significance but criticized its "mechanical heaping up of detail," Buchan
contested modernism's production of "vast shapeless works which were
simply a rubbish-heap of stuff which they believed they had dug out of the
subconscious," maintaining instead that "[u]nrationalised instincts must
find a place in a rational scheme before they have any serious meaning for
literature" (*CO* 255, 256).[16]

In spite of his explicit critique of modernist writing (discussed in my
previous chapter), Buchan's memoirs as written in *Memory Hold-the-Door*
seemingly draw on the very experimentalism they so distinctively reject.
As the book's title signals, *Memory Hold-the-Door* is a text built out of
reminiscences rather than unmediated "facts," in this way highlighting the
contingencies of Buchan's recollections from the outset. This is not a book
in which past events are presented to the reader as they "actually" occurred
but as Buchan looked back upon them in the last months of his long and
hectic life. *Memory Hold-the-Door* follows a chronological pattern,
broadly speaking, but its narrative flits between events in such a manner as
to enrich its historical tapestry and partially disorientate the reader's sense
of the order in which Buchan's life-experiences took place, leading to
something of a potpourri of memories described by one unsympathetic
reviewer as "'a gallery of unrelated portraits, much incidental description

---

[16] Wyndham Lewis, *Time and Western Man* (1927), ed. Paul Edwards (Santa Rosa:
Black Sparrow Press, 1993), 73.

of landscape; and sundry moral reflections'" (Lownie, *PC* 284). Buchan's depiction of his memory of time spent in America as presenting "the American scene as it appears to one observer—a point of view which does not claim to be that mysterious thing, objective truth" (*MHD* 259) could well be applied to the representational mode of *Memory Hold-the-Door* as a whole.[17] The book's Preface is unequivocal on this point. Invoking Henry James' description of memory as "the irresistible reconstruction, to the all too baffled vision, of irrevocable presences and aspects, the conscious, shining, mocking void, sad somehow with excess of serenity," Buchan notes that *Memory Hold-the-Door* stands for "a journal of certain experiences, not written in the experiencing moment, but rebuilt out of memory" (*MHD* 7), "a record of the impressions made upon me by the outer world, rather than a weaving of such impressions into a personal religion and philosophy" (*MHD* 8). Impressions of this kind, Buchan suggests, are fleeting, ethereal, a view supported by his claim that "this world of recollection demands gentle handling. It is brittle, like all spiritual things. If too coarsely approached the bloom will be rubbed off it like the down on a butterfly's wing" (*MHD* 276).

Buchan's reference to "impressions," a word that appears throughout this text, suggests that *Memory Hold-the-Door* draws on, even if it does not fully conform to, an expressly twentieth-century style of autobiography which discloses "a tendency not only to see one's own life as a work of art, but also to be conscious of the act of telling it as drawing on the resources of art."[18] Compare Buchan's idiom with Ford Madox Ford's. Ford writes in *Ancient Lights* (1911) that the book "is full of inaccuracies as to facts, but its accuracy as to impressions is absolute," and in *Return to Yesterday* (1931) he notes that his memories amount to a "novel" describing a life that "meanders, jumps back and forwards, draws netted patterns like those on the musk melon."[19] Approximating something similar to Ford's autobiographical language, Buchan evokes the constructedness of memory, the impossibility of an Archimedean or "objective" point of view, and the need for autobiography to resist

---

[17] Note that Janet Adam Smith suggests that *Memory Hold-the-Door* "was to present [Buchan's] public face; the tone was to be calm and reflective" (Adam Smith, *JB* 462).

[18] Max Saunders, "Biography and Autobiography," in Laura Marcus and Peter Nicholls, eds, *The Cambridge History of Twentieth-Century English Literature* (Cambridge: Cambridge University Press, 2005), 286-303, at 294.

[19] Ford Madox Hueffer [Ford], *Ancient Lights and Certain New Reflections Being the Memories of a Young Man* (London: Chapman and Hall, 1911), xv; *Return to Yesterday* (1931), ed. Bill Hutchings (Manchester: Carcanet, 1999), 4 and 5.

suppressing the labyrinthine elements and fullness of lived experience.
Memory Hold-the-Door openly signals its subjectivism and the fallibility
of its insights, a move that enables Buchan "to dwell on the problems of
interpretation."[20] Buchan was no stranger to a conception of the artist-
figure as a recorder of diaphanous, gossamer-like perceptions, a figure he
described in *Scholar Gipsies* (1896) as "the connoisseur of sensations and
impressions," but there are vital differences between his approach to
writing and the impressionism of a Ford.[21] Whereas Ford's aesthetic
emphasized "the opacity and unknowability of other people; the subjective
and often unreliable nature of our cognitions; and the difficulty of making
sense of reality," *Memory Hold-the-Door* exhibits biography within
autobiography, discussing other people more so than its author, and it
offers a reading of post-War modernity seeking to place it within a context
of politics, culture, and theology.[22]

The aesthetic of *Memory Hold-the-Door* arguably might be described
as a "weak" or "alternative" impressionism. But a key point of divergence
here concerns the matter of didacticism, which in Ford's model of
impressionism is refused. As Ford wrote in *The March of Literature*
(1938), the drawing of morals is unnecessary in impressionist prose not
only because it "would take away from the vividness and entirely destroy
the verisimilitude of [a given] scene," but also because, in Ford's view,
properly and impersonally depicted scenes enable readers to draw their
own ethical conclusions.[23] Buchan's *Memory Hold-the-Door*, by contrast,
is full of homiletic moments, whether it be him holding forth on national
identity, the effect of the War upon civilization, or the value of freedom
during an inter-war period of dictatorship and autocracy, for instance (see
MHD 168-9, 166, 180, 287). Buchan's usage of impressions in *Memory
Hold-the-Door* includes analocutions, hesitant ellipses which among other
things serve as markers of irrevocable phenomena, but there is little sense
in this text of profound epistemological doubt, at least of a doubt leading
to interpretative paralysis. On the contrary, *Memory Hold-the-Door* fully
attests the ways in which, at least for Buchan, others *can* be known and

---

[20] Daniell, *The Interpreter's House*, 198. For more on the unreliable qualities of
Memory Hold-the-Door, see Adam Smith, *JB* 148, 175-6. See also Lownie, *PC*
283.
[21] Buchan, *Scholar-Gipsies*, 12.
[22] Andrzej Gasiorek, "Ford Madox Ford's Modernism and the Question of
Tradition," in *English Literature in Transition, 1880-1920* 44: 1 (2001), 3-27, at
13-14.
[23] Ford Madox Ford, *The March of Literature: From Confucius' Day to our Own*
(Normal, IL: Dalkey Archive Press, 1994), 841-2.

given significance. A moment in the text such as Buchan's uncertainty as to how best to represent Arthur Balfour "for those who did not know him" (*MHD* 128) does not amount to a moment of opacity insofar as it does not repudiate *knowability* but, rather, problematizes the *transferral* of knowledge to other selves. Ultimately, Ford and the Buchan of *Memory Hold-the-Door* are furthest apart on the issue of experiential understanding. Buchan's view, articulated at the beginning of *Memory Hold-the-Door*, that youthful experience "can later be recaptured and amplified by memory, so that at leisure we can interpret its meaning and enjoy its savour" (*MHD* 7), is far indeed from the Ford who noted elsewhere, with Matthew Arnold in mind, that "[w]e may contemplate life steadily enough to-day: it is impossible to see it whole."[24]

It is suggested in *Memory Hold-the-Door* that Buchan's split with Ford's rejection of moral didacticism was rooted in an antipathy towards modernism's apparent ethical disengagement during the immediately post-War period. Buchan wrote that the "War had shown that our mastery over physical forces might end in a nightmare, that mankind was becoming like an overgrown child armed with deadly weapons, a child with immense limbs and a tiny head" (*MHD* 183). However, he pointed out that, in his view, this "belated enlightenment seemed to drain their vitality," with "their" here referring to the literary intelligentsia, "the people who should have influenced opinion" who instead "ran round their cages in vigorous pursuit of their tails" (*MHD* 183). In what is surely a reference to T. S. Eliot, Buchan argued that "[j]ust as many of the boys then leaving school, who had escaped war service, suffered from a kind of *accidie* and were inclined to look for 'soft options' in life, so the interpreting class plumed themselves wearily on being hollow men living in a waste land" (*MHD* 183-4). Intellectuals had to face a post-War modernity in which Enlightenment ideals of rationality and progress had come unstuck, and in some quarters, Buchan argued, this gave rise to peculiarly unrefined notions of history. These included those evinced in Lytton Strachey's historical biographies, at one extreme, and religious and political fanaticism, such as the drift of many intellectuals towards authoritarianism, at the other. Moreover, Buchan contended that the intelligentsia at this time admitted "no absolute values, being by profession atomisers, engaged in reducing the laborious structure of civilised life to a whirling nebula" (*MHD* 184).[25] Buchan himself had been a philosophical relativist since

---

[24] Ford Madox Hueffer [Ford], *The Critical Attitude* (London: Duckworth, 1911), 28

[25] Buchan revered the intellect, but he was certainly critical of intellectuality-for-intellectuality's-sake, opting instead for a moderate account of balance in which rationality ought to be tempered by intuition. In this respect, the views expressed in

reading Arthur Balfour in his youth, but there is a world of difference
between a relativism such as Buchan's, which describes the status of
knowledge (which emphasizes, as Stanley Fish puts it "that foundations
are local and temporal phenomena, and are always vulnerable to
challenges from other localities and other times"), and the intellectual
relativism to which he accused the modernist literati of subscribing.[26] By
means of various disintegrative emphases, as Buchan saw it, such a
relativism threatened those very value systems through which the post-
War world might be rebuilt.[27]

    Buchan can further be aligned with the modernists in identifying a
general decline in post-War English letters, but the most obvious sign of
difference between them is that he laid the blame for that decline on the
doorstep of modernism itself. Buchan's explanation for this decline was
twofold and interdependent: first, he detected a salaciousness or "dull
farmyard candour" in literature chiefly associated with the Joycean
highlighting of bodily functions, one that led to "irrelevant" forms of
coarseness; and second, for Buchan this "all spelled a revolt against
humanism, a return to the sourness of puritanism without its discipline and
majesty" (*MHD* 186). Unlike Renaissance humanism—which, as Buchan
conceived it, centralized "man," had faith in social "progress," and set
great store by the prospect of Arcadia—the "new rebels did not greatly
admire humanity, seeing chiefly its animal grossness, they did not believe
in progress, and they had no high-pitched dreams of a coming golden age"
(*MHD* 186-7), leading to rootlessness, melancholia, and disorder. Buchan
conceded that his "intelligence admitted the merit of much that filled the
rest of [him] with *ennui*," and he expressed a dislike for the "hothouse
world" of Marcel Proust's *In Search of Lost Time* (1913-27) even if in
Buchan's view "it was idle to deny [Proust's] supreme skill in disentangling

---

Craw's article, written half-way through *Castle Gay*, are close to Buchan's own:
"Its subject was the value of the simple human instincts, too often overlaid by the
civilised, the essential wisdom of the plain man. Just as a prophet must sojourn
occasionally into the wilderness, so it was right for culture now and then to rub
shoulders with simplicity" (*CG* 144).
[26] Stanley Fish, *Doing What Comes Naturally: Change, Rhetoric, and the Practice
of Theory in Literary and Legal Studies* (Durham: Duke University Press, 1989),
30. For Buchan's relativism, see *MHD* 39, and "Truth and Accuracy" (1932),
Buchan Papers, National Library of Scotland, Acc. 11627, Box 31/4, 19-20, 15.
[27] Note that Buchan and Fish cannot wholly be aligned on the point of relativism,
however, as in Buchan's notion that principles equate to "eternal and universal
truth[s]" (*CO* 124). For Fish's repudiation of the entire category of "principles,"
see *The Trouble With Principle* (Cambridge, MA: Harvard University Press,
1999).

subtle threads of thought and emotion," but he ultimately asserted that the merits of such textualities (merits which in this text Buchan left unspecified) "were beyond doubt, but their method and the whole world which they represented seemed to me ineffably dismal" (*MHD* 201).

Buchan's world at this time was one focussed on memories and impressions; a reality of mind and mood rather than of materiality. In *Memory Hold-the-Door* he explores his own recollections and psychology, and in this regard it represents a kind of textual fulfilment of his view, advanced in 1935, that "[i]n a very real sense there are no frontiers left on the physical map. They must be sought in the world of the mind and the spirit" (*CO* 10). This was a perspective in long gestation. Buchan wrote in his Preface to *The Last Secrets: The Final Mysteries of Exploration* (1923) that "[t]here are no more unvisited forbidden cities, or unapproached high mountains, or unrecorded great rivers," adding: "It is in a high degree improbable that many geographical problems remain, the solving of which will come upon the mind with the overwhelming romance of the unveilings we have been privileged to witness."[28] However, even then he pointed out that "mystery" itself, "[t]he Unknown, happily, will be always with us, for there are infinite secrets in a blade of grass, and an eddy of wind, and a grain of dust, and human knowledge will never attain that finality when the sense of wonder shall cease."[29] In the posthumously published *Sick Heart River* (1941) Buchan returns to this point in quite some detail, repeating the diagnosis itself through Clifford Savory, who suggests that America "'is up against the biggest problem in her history. It is not a single question like slavery or state rights, or the control of monopolies, or any of the straightforward things that have made a crisis before. It is a conglomeration of problems, most of which we cannot define. We have no geographical frontier left, but we've an eternal frontier in our minds'" (*SHR* 35). Mentality itself here becomes the great unknown, the final wilderness to survey and investigate. At the end of Buchan's life it was psychology, explored and charted here by means of alternative techniques to the subjectivist modernisms his work antagonized, that came into the ascendant.[30]

Sick Heart River begins with an Edward Leithen much changed since his appearance in *The Power-House*. Frail and dying from tuberculosis, as

---

[28] Buchan, *The Last Secrets: The Final Mysteries of Exploration* (London: Thomas Nelson, 1923), vii-viii.

[29] *Ibid.*, vii.

[30] Thus Buchan in *Memory Hold-the-Door*: "As we grow older we escape from the tyranny of matter and recognise that the true centre of gravity is in the mind" (*MHD* 291).

well as aware of the insufficiencies of a "physical shell" (*SHR* 15) lived
not in sports and athletics but in legal analysis, Leithen is visited by
Blenkiron, the old friend of Hannay and Sandy Arbuthnot. Blenkiron's
niece's husband, Francis Galliard, has gone missing, and Blenkiron,
unaware of Leithen's delicate condition, has come to offer Leithen the
chance to "'piece together the bits that make up the jigsaw puzzle'" (*SHR*
18). While initially taken aback by the proposal, Leithen agrees and sets
off for New York to pick up Galliard's trail. We are informed that for
Leithen this assignment had initially "been no more than a peg on which to
hang a private determination, an excuse, partly to himself and partly to the
world, for a defiant finish to his career" (*SHR* 39). And yet, as Leithen is
drawn further into the intrigue (and meets the human agents of this affair)
the task becomes something more significant, just as Francis himself shifts
in Leithen's mind's-eye from "a disembodied ghost, a mere premise in an
argument" (*SHR* 39) and "shadow" (*SHR* 40) to a human subject who must
be located and brought back to safety.[31] Going back to the structure of *The
Power-House*—which begins, as we saw in Chapter Three, with Leithen
being informed of the disappearance of Charles Pitt-Heron—*Sick Heart
River* transposes Leithen's involvement in a human drama not only onto a
larger platform but also into a more intimate *and* cosmic set of
significances.[32] Searching for Galliard out in the wild, Leithen comes to
recognize his journey as the march to spiritual self-realization: "He felt
that in this strange place he was passing, while still in time, inside the
bounds of eternity. He was learning to know himself, and with that might
come the knowledge of God" (*SHR* 77). Leithen's death, in turn, is read by
others (*SHR* 208-9) as the achievement of a new kind of life obtainable
only via "hallowed" insight.

Buchan's usage of the word "shadow" in the quotation above
establishes an image that resonates throughout this text. Shadows are
emblems of secondary relation wherein something exists proportionate to
another, more substantive thing. The much-observed parallels between
Leithen and Buchan are one element of this body of relations, but one of
two key affinities in *Sick Heart River* is the link between Leithen and

---

[31] Leithen comes to recognize that "Galliard was no longer a mathematical symbol,
a cipher in a game, but a human being and Felicity's husband" (*SHR* 133).
[32] This cosmic accenting recurs in the later stages of Leithen's journey: "In his old
bustling world there were the works of man's hands all around to give a false
impression of man's power. But here the hand of God had blotted out life for
millions of miles and made a great tract of the inconsiderable ball which was the
earth, like the infinite interstellar spaces which had never heard of man" (*SHR*
114).

Galliard, which is troped as a doubling between two alternatively weakened personages, the one physically diseased, the other mentally unsound. "There was a time limit for Francis Galliard, as there was one for Edward Leithen" (*SHR* 42), we are told. When Leithen finally gets to the arctic snow-fields in which he imagines he will find his goal, he reflects: "Somewhere down in that labyrinth was Galliard. Somewhere down there he would leave his own bones" (*SHR* 85). Leithen's efforts to find Galliard are both a journey from which he himself will not return and an inscription of himself in the "other" he is trying to find. As Leithen moves through the first stages of his quest he "read[s] himself into the soul of Francis Galliard, a summary and provisional reading, but enough to give him a starting point" (*SHR* 48-9). The second key act of shadowing in this text is that between Leithen and the supernatural. Leithen's quest is one that takes place in the physical site of the freezing north-west Canadian wilderness, but it is also very much a transition between worlds during which Leithen comes to understand himself as but part of a greater and sacred frame of reference. *Sick Heart River* contains a number of moments in which Leithen perceives the surrounding wilderness as "wild" only in a limited physical sense, but infinitely plentiful inasmuch as it encompasses the raw grandeur of divine creativity. Father Duplessis' conception of that wild country as a place where "'man is nothing and God is all'" (*SHR* 69) pre-empts Leithen's insights into the encouraging boundlessness of apparent wasteland: "He had been right in doing as he had done, coming out to meet death in a world where death and life were colleagues and not foes. He felt that in this strange place he was passing, while still in time, inside the bounds of eternity" (*SHR* 77).

Sick Heart River thus marks a significant thematic development away from Leithen's first appearance in Buchan's work, the short story "Space" (1910). This brief piece takes the form of a recollection by Leithen, who recounts the tale of his friend Hollond to an unnamed narrator-figure. Hollond, "'an erratic genius'" with an interest in "'the mathematical conception of infinity'" (*SS2* 183), finds inside the apparent emptiness of physical space "'not an empty homogenous medium'" but a realm of immaterial existence "'full of intricate differences, intelligible and real, though not with our common reality'" (*SS2* 187). Hollond's mathematical rationalism gives him access to a non-human realm of the infinite that marks the borderline between the real and the ideal, between materiality and a vertiginous mysticism which ultimately leads him to take his own life while climbing in the Alps. Having picked at the lock of the deepest of worldly enigmas, Hollond becomes saturated by the knowledge of a world with which ordinary, sceptical human existence has no commerce: "'He had seen the something more, the little bit too much, which plucks a man from his moorings. He had gone so far into the land of pure spirit that he must needs go further and shed the fleshly envelope that cumbered him'" (*SS2* 197). Hollond's story serves as an indicator of a spiritualism against which the down-to-earth pragmatics of Leithen and the story's narrator can be measured, for in a sense the real subject of "Space" is their insensitiveness to the true nature of Hollond's discoveries. Leithen dismisses the latter's findings as a form of madness, while the narrator deems Leithen's story to be a "yarn" (*SS2* 195) with no possible purchase on the life-world. But it is precisely in the gap between Hollond's brilliant saneness—evinced by his ability to function in academic debate after his discoveries have been made (*SS2* 193)—and the inflexibility of Leithen and the story's narrator that the story's moral unfolds. Pure spirit, "Space" argues, is everywhere and in everything; it further suggests that there is an inevitable conversion (death, rebirth, psychological change) involved in the very act of discerning that newfound sense of super-reality.

    Buchan's fictions reiterate this insight a number of times, as in the already mentioned spiritual significance of Hannay's movements in *The Thirty-Nine Steps*, but in *Sick Heart River* there is a finality to Leithen's recognitions for which, one feels, Buchan's earlier fictions have busily been preparing. Alan Sandison is surely right in saying that *Sick Heart River* presents a Buchan who has developed significantly from the young writer who penned *The Half-Hearted* to a reflective, elderly writer showing in written form "one man's struggle for communion, one man's honest and unrelenting battle to come to terms with his own particular destiny."[33] Hugh Somerville states in *A Lodge in the Wilderness* that "'[y]ears, you know, bring the philosophic mind, and a certain unity creeps into our life without our knowing it'" (*LW* 214). *Sick Heart River*, by contrast, portrays a philosophic mind in clear spiritual orientation to the wholeness that surrounds it, one that recognizes in natural space an Edenic identity "like a garden in a long-settled land, a garden made centuries ago by the very good and the very wise" (*SHR* 43). To Leithen, this natural topography signifies "a frontier between the desert and the sown," "the borderline between the prosaic world, where things went by rule and rote and were all fitted to the human scale, and the world as God first made it out of chaos, which had no care for humanity" (*SHR* 43). Indeed, the River of the Sick Heart itself conjures up a vision in Leithen's mind of the collapse of this binary into a direct admixture of the heavenly and the material: "It seemed to him that he was looking at the most marvellous

---

[33] Sandison, *The Wheel of Empire*, 190.

spectacle ever vouchsafed to man. The elements were commonplace—
stone and wood, water and earth—but so had been the pigments of a
Raphael. The celestial Demiurge had combined them into a masterpiece"
(*SHR* 105). This sighting of a kind of New Jerusalem, to which the Sick
Heart River is compared on several occasions in the text (*SHR* 74, 99,
119), reinforces Leithen's understanding of the Canadian landscape as a
cipher for the omnipresence of, and human dependence on, divinity: "He
was an atom in infinite space, the humblest of slaves waiting on the
command of an august master" (*SHR* 114).

What has happened here, then, is that *The Power-House*'s resituating
of the imperial frontier to the metropolitan heartland has been transformed
into an analogous transformation of material conflict into spiritual, mental,
and emotional terms.[34] It is perhaps surprising, then, to find that *Sick
Heart River* has been criticized by scholars for these ideological
metamorphoses. For Laurence Kitzan, *Sick Heart River* is a disappointment
precisely insofar as it does not conform to the "unthinking" ideologies of
imperial adventure established elsewhere in Buchan's *oeuvre*:

> Ultimately as an imperial adventure story, *Sick Heart River* is a failure
> because it has become too introspective; it asks too many questions about
> whether this or that action by Leithen is really worth doing, and though it
> does not ask such questions about the empire, it sets the stage for those
> questions to be asked after the immediate crisis of world war. Even though
> the imperial hero saves the Hares from the psychological death-trap in
> which they had become mired, it is all too easy to see that the civilization
> that the empire has brought to these people is in some way responsible for
> their dilemmas. [Buchan's] pre-World War I imperial novels would not
> have asked questions of these kinds, because the values expressed in these
> novels are as yet unchallenged by a major portion of the literate public.
> Therefore, *Sick Heart River* is more satisfying as literature than as a
> defense of the rationale of empire such as Buchan had expounded back in
> 1906 with *A Lodge in the Wilderness*.[35]

In this passage Kitzan offers an insightful perspective on *Sick Heart
River*'s reflective account of the destructive influence of empire upon the
Hare Indians, but the clear answer to his valuation of the novel as a
"failure" is that *Sick Heart River* appears to criticize the imperial adventure

---

[34] This generic shift is mirrored in Leithen's realization that his quest necessitates a
"generic" blurring of his own professional capacities. As he says to Blenkiron:
"'You want a combination of detective, psychologist, and sportsman'" (*SHR* 18).
[35] Laurence Kitzan, *Victorian Writers and the Image of Empire: The Rose-Colored
Vision* (Westport, CT: Greenwood Press, 2001), 180.

story narrative mode to which Buchan so often turned. Consequently, to fault the novel for not following in the tradition of a genre which it carefully refashions is somewhat redundant. *Sick Heart River* moves away from the world of *The Power-House* and *John Macnab*—a world of rational thought and material phenomena—towards a spiritual realm characterized by self-questioning. Leithen's deliberative intelligence, the jurisprudential strengths of which are still much in evidence (for example, *SHR* 49), is now turned against the deliberator, in a text which displaces the "true" metropolitan adventure of *The Power-House* into the still truer quest for self-knowledge.

The doubts and questioning to which Leithen exposes himself have a wide set of ramifications. As an imperial subject, to interrogate the relationship between self and world is to consider also the relationship between that self and the alterity against which it must necessarily be defined. *Sick Heart River*'s principal source of otherness lies in the Hare Indians with whom, it is suggested, Leithen has a powerful emotive bond (*SHR* 104). In this sense the text offers a further kind of doubling between "the Hare people [who] would presently die" (*SHR* 103) and Leithen, whose recuperation enables him to prevent their own demise from "'a dreadful *accidie* which makes them impotent and without hope'" (*SHR* 160). Leithen's initial unconcern with that beyond himself—"His inner world was crumbling so fast that he had lost any craving for permanence in the externals of life" (*SHR* 7)—is translated through the reconstitution of that inner world into a genuine concern for the other that facilitates its continued existence. At first indifferent to the "future of a few hundred degenerate Indians who mattered not at all in his scheme of things" (*SHR* 164), the knowledge of the world having fallen into world war yet again prompts Leithen into action: "It might be the twilight of the gods, the end of all things. The globe might swim in blood. Death might resume his ancient reign. But, by Heaven, he would strike his blow for life, even a pitiful flicker of it" (*SHR* 183). In the end, it is the duplicated failure of the Enlightenment ideals through which the ideology of imperial adventure is articulated that spurs Leithen on, and by providing the Hares with food he finishes the "plain task before him, to fight with Death" (*SHR* 187).[36]

Leithen's death from myocarditis (*SHR* 197)—inflammation of the muscular sections of the heart—did not parallel Buchan's own passing in

---

[36] Leithen's envisioning of the failure of Enlightenment takes the form of a Europe plunged into chaos and barbarity: "He saw Europe as a carnage pit—shattered towns, desecrated homes, devastated cornlands, roads blocked with the instruments of war—the meadows of France and of Germany, and of his own kind England" (*SHR* 187).

1940, which followed a cerebral blood clot that led to a fall, unconsciousness, trepanation, and eventual death (Adam Smith, *JB* 470). However, there are some heartening correspondences between the two lives. Leithen's death is widely reported; Buchan's was of a global and across-the-board import. George VI telegraphed Buchan's wife shortly after he succumbed, where he stated that "'[h]is loss will be widely mourned and his name, both as an eminent author and a distinguished Governor-General long remembered and esteemed'" (quoted in Lownie, *PC* 280). Leithen's extensive network of friends was matched in Buchan's own massive circle of comrades, acquaintances, and dear companions, a good many of whom he had earlier lost in the First World War. Of that appalling bereavement Buchan wrote: "I do not believe that the relation between human beings called friendship can be rated too high."[37] What Buchan wrote of Leithen in *Sick Heart River* the author would perhaps have felt applicable to himself: "He had survived the War, when the best of his contemporaries had fallen in swathes. He had been amazingly successful in his profession and had enjoyed every moment of his work. Honours had fallen to him out of all proportion to his merits. He had had a thousand pleasures—books, travel, the best of sport, the best of friends" (*SHR* 13).

---

[37] Buchan, *These for Remembrance*, unpaginated.

CHAPTER SEVEN

CONCLUSION:
SECRET AGENCIES

In this book I have attempted several things: to introduce readers to a more or less delineative summary of Buchan's fictional and non-fictional work; to make *evaluative* comments about that work; and to make a case for Buchan as a *modern* writer whose texts engage with the early twentieth-century environment within which they emerged. In doing so, I have made no claims to comprehensiveness. This book, inevitably, is a partial one. Buchan, in my view, remains significant for two key reasons. First, because his writing offers us another point of view on the ideological, technological, and cultural developments of the Edwardian and post-First World War epochs. Buchan's perspective has been received as a "popular," middlebrow approach, but we should not equate such an approach, I have argued, with the feeble abilities bestowed upon so-called "popular" writing by Leavisite cultural historians. Buchan's texts enable us to see that the serious/popular binary cannot fully account for the ways in which popular writing not only engages with history but is often directly and productively involved in its developments. Second, I have taken some pains to show that Buchan should not be marked off from the modernisms against which literary history has placed him. He was no modernist, of course, but he read and evaluated modernism in ways that may now seem surprising. It is for this reason, in part, that Buchan ought to be studied by serious scholars of the late-Victorian, early twentieth-century, and inter-war socio-literary cultures. His work needs to be seen as part of a dialectic that involves exchange and opposition between popular forms and modernist elitisms, elitisms that themselves were often based upon fashionable modes of experience. Buchan's modernity, as much as James Joyce's or T. S. Eliot's, lies in his recognition that the modern world was not something from which to shy away, but an actuality that demanded frank examination and analysis.

Buchan's attempts at such an analysis roughly can be divided into four periods: the early work of empire, which runs from the Edwardian *fin de siècle* up to around 1910; the immediately pre-War and First World War phase, in which Buchan's mastery of the thriller form took shape; the post-War epoch up to approximately 1930, a time which was for Buchan one of coming to terms with unprecedentedly violent social and cultural upheavals; and the years between 1930 and his death, during which Buchan wrote some of his most experimental and introspective literary fictions. One central dynamic across all these periods is the idea of empire. From *The Half-Hearted* (1900) to *Sick Heart River* (1941) it is the linked questions and challenges of empire, imperialism, and colonialism to which Buchan consistently turns. If novels and semi-novels such as *A Lodge in the Wilderness* (1906) and *Prester John* (1910) deal with far-flung imperial frontiers, then it is in the wartime thrillers—*The Power-House* (1913), *The Thirty-Nine Steps* (1915), *Greenmantle* (1916), and *Mr Standfast* (1919)—that the idea of the imperial frontier as "consciousness," as the dividing line between barbarism and civilization, is relocated to the imperial homeland. In these fictions it is the threat posed by global intrigue to individual psychology that matters as much as the dangers targeted at territory and military holdings. In their different ways, Buchan's texts as a whole explore these linked dividing lines by means of a range of literary modes, from the comical and romantic—*Huntingtower* (1922)—to the experimental and gargantuan—*The Courts of the Morning* (1929). In all these texts the idea of history looms large, whether as disclosed by Buchan's intimidating knowledge of facts and times gone by, or as revealed in his use of the historical romance in works such as *Witch Wood* (1927), which unites a strong historical attitude, a committed social conscience, and an erudite literary technique.

Throughout this book I've urged a sympathetic view of Buchan's relationships with his modernist contemporaries. One reason for doing so is that I think his work should be read as an historical example of how modernism was received in its time. The now-receding view of modernism as neatly cordoned-off from the various Edwardian and Georgian textualities that writers such as Virginia Woolf disparaged is challenged in Buchan's writing. His essays, which I have emphasized here as central to his achievement, are key in this respect. Pieces such as "The Old and the New in Literature" (1925) and *The Novel and the Fairy Tale* (1931) indicate that a "popular" writer could indeed take an authoritatively critical stance against modernist experimentation and at the same time gesture towards a more subtle reconciliation between written forms such as the thriller and the experimentalisms they were thought to antagonize. Buchan remains worthy of our attention precisely because his work unsettles received views of literary history. *Memory Hold-the-Door* (1940) is in a variety of senses a traditionally-written autobiography, but as I have suggested it can be thought of as a crossover point to the more self-reflexive autobiographical styles favoured by writers such as Ford Madox Ford, Wyndham Lewis, and H. G. Wells, among many others. Richard Remington's view, in Wells's *The New Machiavelli* (1911), that "[a]rt is selection and so is most autobiography" is centrally and self-reflexively dealt with in Buchan's own life history.[1] Likewise, for all their occasional simplicities, Buchan's literary texts again and again make use of the *lack* of closure championed by modernist novels, something that we can observe only by closely attending to the nuances of Buchan's output as a whole.

Buchan's approach to the craft of fiction-writing reflects a superbly intelligent and complex worldview, one that is only partially revealed within the materials I have been discussing. In this study I have tried to demonstrate, where possible, how Buchan's literary work links up with his non-fictional commentaries, histories, biographies, and essays, but another study could easily be written on these works of gentlemanly scholarship alone. Buchan's polymathic character makes it difficult to encompass the wide variety of his opinions by attending to a single branch of his output; there are, in a sense, as many Buchans as relate to the numerous interests he pursued and excelled at throughout his life, and his rate of textual production reflects this many-sided exuberance. As William Buchan once wrote, his father started to write "when he was not much over sixteen years old; when he died at sixty five he had completed more than fifty volumes, and he was writing five books at once when death overtook him."[2] Buchan himself noted: "I have always tried to have one or two subjects on hand on which I worked, and which engaged a different part of oneself from that which was employed in earning one's bread" (*CO* 171). That Buchan coupled literary success with broad publication in a range of disciplines is evidence of a keen mind and meticulous organization, two elements that, in different ways, play key roles in the worlds Buchan chose to depict in his fiction. There are positive kinds of planning in Buchan, usually evinced by those figures who attend to life's anarchies through what he saw as the largely benign activities of lawyers, "clean" propagandists, soldiers, and adventurers, among others. But Buchan's mind was always in tune with the darker accompaniments to such professions, and accordingly his fiction is filled with harmful schemers and malign systems, individuals who remake the world from undetected

---

[1] H. G. Wells, *The New Machiavelli* (1911), ed. Simon J. James (London: Penguin, 2005), 316.

[2] William Buchan, *The "Wreath'd Trellis"*, 12.

places in accordance with radical ideologies. In the remainder of this concluding chapter I briefly want to consider some of these alternative manifestations of "orderliness" in Buchan's fiction with regard to their most common symptoms: suspiciousness, pathology, and paranoia.

In saying this, I do not mean to suggest that the dominant psychological mode of Buchan's *life* was a paranoid view of reality. But I would suggest that there is a sufficient quantity of paranoid nuances in his fictional works to warrant finding in that *oeuvre* a recurrent suspiciousness, one that, as we will see, both challenges and reinforces its own pathological framework. One should be precise here. The view of Buchan's work I have in mind works on two interrelated levels. The first level is that of the psychopathology of Buchan's characters. A good example of this is the following insight of Leithen's in *The Power-House*: "You know the feeling that someone is watching you, a sort of sensation which the mind receives without actual evidence. If the watcher is behind, where you can't see him, you have a cold feeling between your shoulders. I daresay it is a legacy from the days when the cave-man had to look pretty sharp to keep from getting his enemy's knife between the ribs" (*PH* 43). *Castle Gay*'s term for this—"'persecution-mania'" (*CG* 66)—is an appropriate one: time and again, Buchan's characters fear that they are being followed, imagine themselves to be of (ostensibly) unwarranted significance, project their own failings onto others, become aggressive, and visualize themselves as powerless creatures adrift in unsympathetic worlds. In *Prester John*, David Crawfurd's references to "perpetual spying" (*PJ* 39), to a feeling that he alone can thwart an indefinable peril (*PJ* 61), and to a silent, unseen espionage (*PJ* 37) are early confirmations of a mindset that recurs throughout Buchan's work.

The second level is that of the ontology of the text itself, its significance as an expression of culture. This level is concerned with the paranoid identities of texts as cultural objects, how they programme the fears of the communities from which they emerge, and how they strive to contain the threats by means of which those anxieties come into being. Buchan's thrillers are key in this regard, since the thriller form itself has routinely been interpreted by scholars as a literary mode dependent on a paranoid conception of experience.[3] *The Three Hostages* contains a good example of this level of the text in Dr Greenslade's opinions regarding post-war civilization. Greenslade's views adumbrate both the specific

---

[3] For the paranoia of the thriller see Jerry Palmer, *Thrillers: Genesis and Structure of a Popular Genre* (London: Edward Arnold, 1978), 86, and Michael Denning, *Cover Stories: Narrative and Ideology in the British Spy Thriller* (London: Routledge and Kegan Paul, 1987), 41.

social diagnosis of *The Three Hostages* and point to the nature of the thriller-textuality within which that diagnosis is articulated:

> All history has been an effort to make definitions, clear rules of thought, clear rules of conduct, solid sanctions, by which we can conduct our life. These are the work of the conscious self. The subconscious is an elementary and lawless thing. If it intrudes on life two results must follow. There will be a weakening of the power of reasoning, which, after all, is the thing that brings men nearest to the Almighty. And there will be a failure of nerve. (*TH* 15)

The meta-textual elements of this passage are twofold. On the one hand this account describes a fusion of the rational and subliminal worlds necessitated by the thriller protagonist's essentially paranoid responses to reality.[4] On the other it captures the generic negotiations of the thriller itself as a mechanism of cultural engagement. For what else is the genre if not an attempt to protect "solid" narratives of meaning from the anarchies of the world "out there"? The thriller's sense of reality—its "paranoid imaginary"—is reflected in its very form, its attribution of apparently random occurrences to a conspiratorial other translated into the genre's view of history as a complex of clandestine intentions, secrecies, and malevolent surveillances.

Freud's account of paranoia is instructive in this regard. Despite his interest in paranoia as a vehicle for the signification of repressed homosexuality, it is clear that his theory is primarily architectonic: it replaces chaos with structure, lawlessness with form. The paranoiac, burdened with feelings of smallness or insignificance, "projects" these feelings onto his environment to create an external persecuting agency that only he can detect and defeat. This process of projection has two consequences: it develops the paranoiac into a person of sufficient importance to be worthy of such persecution, eliminating his original feelings of inconsequentiality in the process, and it not only gives to the paranoiac a restored world but also an imaginary uniqueness in which he is bestowed with powers unavailable to others and which only he can use effectively. As Robert Robins and Jerrold Post rightly maintain, he "who returns from the edge of psychological disintegration experiences a

---

[4] In this sense, Crawfurd's claim in *Prester John* that "I would suddenly be conscious, as I walked on the road, that I was being watched" (*PJ* 37) is not entirely accurate: in a true sense, having become paranoid, having moved into a state in which the rational and the subliminal overlap, he is now more unconscious than wakeful.

purification, an ecstatic new world. In a state of euphoria, the patient has reconstituted himself through a grand scheme that centres on him."[5] In this process randomness is replaced with method, chance with "sense": awful emotions are not arbitrary but *designed*, originating elsewhere. Freud himself stated that paranoia is a constructive disorder in which grandeur and centrality *rebuild*: "*The delusional formation, which we take to be the pathological product, is in reality an attempt at recovery, a process of reconstruction.*"[6]

The key factor here, though, is that the attributes of centrality and grandiosity which enable the paranoiac to function in social life are in fact false. Paranoia is self-authorizing, but this validation is obtained at the price of reality. In a clinical sense this means that if the paranoid mentality is unsettled then the whole house of cards comes crashing down, often leading to further illness and, in some instances, suicidal depression. Freud's delusional formation is disrupted, removing the support of fantasy and bringing about internal breakdown. It is a preventative logic in which "what was abolished internally returns from without" by means of a falsifying but beneficial process.[7] Projection, that is, authenticates inauthenticity; it regulates the fantastic through enchanted denial. The primary stimulus of illness is not directly confronted but dispersed outwards to return in an incommensurable form. As Freud notes:

> An internal perception is suppressed, and, instead, its content, after undergoing a certain kind of distortion, enters consciousness in the form of an external perception. In delusions of persecution the distortion consists in a transformation of affect; what should have been felt internally as love is perceived externally as hate.[8]

This new perception is contestable and "othered" but, finally, merely an extension of the self and its failures. It is an artificial scaffold, a false reconstruction or architecture mobilized on shifting sands.

What happens, then, when a text "about" paranoia at the level of character is itself symptomatic of a larger, collective paranoid concern? What is going on in such onion-esque, Russian doll-like productions? One

---

[5] Robert S. Robins and Jerrold M. Post, *Political Paranoia: The Psychopolitics of Hatred* (New Haven: Yale University Press, 1997), 81-2.

[6] Sigmund Freud, "Psycho-Analytic Notes on an Autobiographical Account of a Case of Paranoia (Dementia Paranoides)," in *The Standard Edition of the Complete Psychological Works of Sigmund Freud*, ed. James Strachey *et al*, 24 vols (1953-74) (London: Vintage, 2001), xii, 71, original emphasis.

[7] *Ibid.*

[8] *Ibid.*, 66.

answer to these questions is that the "real" paranoia of the text's interaction with its historical moment contradicts the regenerative or otherwise reconstructive properties of the paranoia exhibited at that same text's narrative level. This is a fundamental tension, discernible not just in Buchan's work but also in a host of other fictions which adhere to the same structure. The "double layering" of a text such as, for instance, *The Thirty-Nine Steps* (paranoia within paranoia) is self-undermining: here, paranoia cannot simply be interpreted as "beneficial" because the paranoid framework within which it is mobilized necessarily renders it false. Thus, although it seems as if paranoia is being seen in this text and others as the means to personal and national salvation, there is a deeper, more vital, *material* unease at work here which disallows any such means to repair. The achievement of Hannay seems effective only because the narrative paranoia producing him as a character makes his success appear certain, a success that is as much the marking of a root problem as it is its alleged resolution or end-point. What transpires in *The Thirty-Nine Steps* is not just that paranoia may prove profitable within certain contexts and under precise conditions, but, more tellingly, that this belief in the use-value of paranoia is already polluted by the mindset it would attempt, leap and bound, to surmount. The paranoia of this text does not signal a pathway towards renewal as much as it does the necessarily traumatized characteristics of this system of belief. As a sign of wider problems, any idea of regenerative possibility the text itself seems to encourage is already part of this logic.

Certainly, the complexities of Buchan's fictional deployment of paranoia can best be seen in his most famous work. *The Thirty-Nine Steps* is a text populated by valetudinarians. Throughout, if its protagonists are not wounded they are nauseous, diseased, or mentally unsound. Famously written while Buchan himself was in bed recovering from a duodenal ulcer, the text begins with Hannay admitting that England's weather made him "liverish" and that the talk of ordinary Englishmen made him "sick" (*TNS* 7). Hangovers are commonplace: an "old potato-digger [who] seemed to have turned peevish" buries his "frowsy head into the cushions" (*TNS* 29) of a railway carriage; an intoxicated roadman can think of nothing but his "fuddled brain" (*TNS* 51); and one of the Black Stone conspirators uses inebriation as an alibi (*TNS* 106). There is reference to "'influenza at Blackpool'" (*TNS* 42), "'colic'" (*TNS* 53), and Hannay is subsequently laid up by a ten day stretch of malaria: "it was a baddish go, and though I was out of bed in five days, it took me some time to get my legs again" (*TNS* 74). Even the political head of the Admiralty is convalescing at Sheringham (*TNS* 84), and Franklin P. Scudder, upon whom so much depends, is referred to as gripped by a "mania" (*TNS* 80) for covering his tracks, while Hannay thinks him a "madman" (*TNS* 9).

Like Buchan's early short story "A Captain of Salvation" (1896), *The Thirty-Nine Steps* offers a vision of the cityscape that hints at a dark underbelly to its seemingly carefree world of tea parties at the houses of "Imperialist ladies" (*TNS* 7) and "shop-girls and clerks and dandies and policemen" who "had some interest in life that kept them going" (*TNS* 8). In this text, London is a site of decadent ruling-class abandon inhabited by exotic revolutionaries and degenerate bodies. Scudder's valet is "a whining fellow with a churchyard face" (*TNS* 16). There is a sense of illness about Hannay's milkman, "a young man ... with an ill-nourished moustache" (*TNS* 22). Loafers shuffle through back streets (*TNS* 23) and men in well-thought-of apartment blocks are murdered by heartless politicos (*TNS* 18). For Hannay, an immigrant himself, London is an alienating, defamiliarizing locality that isolates and estranges more than it nourishes and sustains: "I returned from the City about three o'clock on that May afternoon pretty well disgusted with life" (*TNS* 7), he says. Above all the metropolis is a place of suffocating tedium: "The weather made me liverish, [...] I couldn't get enough exercise, and the amusements of London seemed as flat as soda-water that has been standing in the sun" (*TNS* 7). Indeed, one of the most damaging effects of the city in *The Thirty-Nine Steps* is that it breeds a nihilism grounded in boredom which devalues the individual self's linkage to its locale. Like the beggar he encounters on his way home—"a fellow-sufferer" (*TNS* 8)—boredom marks the emptiness of Hannay's life during his time in London, a futility that leads him to make a vow at Oxford Circus: "I would give the Old Country another day to fit me into something; if nothing happened, I would take the next boat for the Cape" (*TNS* 8).[9] However, this boredom is short-lived: Scudder is murdered, and once Hannay learns of his demise, and subsequently realizes that, since he is in the know, he too must now go on the run, the boredom of the city evaporates: "I reminded myself that a week ago I had been finding the world dull" (*TNS* 24), he notes. Scudder's termination both injects Hannay's existence with the most primitive of meanings (to survive), and, in swapping the city for the restorative potential of the Scots moors, affords him with a rejuvenated awareness of

---

[9] See also Leithen in *John Macnab*, a character for whom, initially at least, "[e]verything seemed weary and over-familiar – the summer smell of town, the din of traffic, the panorama of faces, pretty women shopping, the occasional sight of a friend. Long ago, he reflected with disgust, there had been a time when he had enjoyed it all" (*John Macnab*, 4).

self: "the slackness of the past months was slipping from my bones, and I stepped out like a four-year-old" (*TNS* 27).

That said, in *The Thirty-Nine Steps* bodies fare little better outside the city than they do within its boundaries. If at times the countryside regenerates Hannay, then at others it threatens to smother and engulf him. Looking across a vista he discerns that "at other times I would have liked the place, but now it seemed to suffocate me. The free moorlands were prison walls, and the keen hill air was the breath of a dungeon" (*TNS* 49). In this text, rural space endangers as much as it shelters. Hannay crashes a car on a country road and is chased by airborne spies, of which he comments: "I did not like this espionage from the air, and I began to think less well of the countryside I had chosen for a refuge" (*TNS* 31). During his escape from the bald archaeologist's country mansion, Hannay is injured by the explosive he uses to blast his way out of the house: "Nausea shook me, and a wheel in my head kept turning, while my left shoulder and arm seemed to be stricken with the palsy" (*TNS* 68). His limbs aching "like hell" (*TNS* 68), he climbs onto a dovecot where he proceeds "to go off into an old-fashioned swoon" (*TNS* 69). Indeed, Hannay's injuries are worse than he at first realizes: "Those lentonite fumes had fairly poisoned me, and the baking hours on the dovecot hadn't helped matters. I had a crushing headache, and felt as sick as a cat. Also my shoulder was in a bad way. At first I thought it was only a bruise, but it seemed to be swelling, and I had no use of my left arm" (*TNS* 72). No less so than the metropolitan byways, the rural is figured here as a site of jeopardy and, supplemented by automobiles, aeroplanes, and dynamite, a place of technological risk.

Consequently, *The Thirty-Nine Steps* goes against Allan Hepburn's view that the spy thriller celebrates technology as an extension and intensification of the spy's invincibility.[10] The point to make here is not that Hannay's capabilities are solely hampered by the various technologies he encounters, but, rather, that *The Thirty-Nine Steps* emphasizes the inseparability of prosthesis and pathology. Using Buchan's work as one of his examples, Hepburn accurately contends that in the spy thriller "[t]echnology makes human eyes, ears, and limbs more powerful by leaving an impression of the spy's ubiquity," but if a basic consequence of bodily enhancement is an empowered self, then one of its disturbing implications is an acknowledgement of the body's radical impermanence: bodies that can be augmented are also bodies that can putrefy and fall

---

[10] Allan Hepburn, *Intrigue: Espionage and Culture* (New Haven: Yale University Press, 2005), 15.

apart.[11] Technological prosthesis is qualified by pathological response in *The Thirty-Nine Steps*, a good example being Hannay's "sickening plunge" (*TNS* 41) during his car crash: here, auto-mobility is at once auto-infirmity. Another is Hannay's queasy reaction to the "dense and acrid fog" (*TNS* 67) produced during his explosive getaway. But perhaps the most interesting convergence of prosthesis and pathology in *The Thirty-Nine Steps* emerges in what is the novel's most conspicuous, and most conspicuously nameless, form of psychological malady: paranoia. Indeed, Hannay's paranoia is a pathology that approaches prosthesis insofar as it artificially enhances his ability to interpret the phenomenal world by attributing meaning to unconnected events.

And yet, in what sense Hannay can be thought of as paranoid is a key critical question. The evidence is ambiguous. Hannay is forced into unconsciousness by the sheer power of the dynamite he detonates at the conspirators' headquarters (*TNS* 67), but in a very true sense he spends the majority of the narrative in an "unconscious" state in which private fantasy and external reality are impossible to tell apart. This "fantasy within a fantasy," as Nicholas Hiley terms it, bears all the hallmarks of paranoid logic (suspicion, centrality, grandiosity, hostility, fear of loss of autonomy, projection, and delusional thinking), a logic that begins to determine Hannay's activities after he finds Scudder's corpse.[12] "The men who knew that he knew what he knew had found him, and had taken the best way to make certain of his silence. Yes; but he had been in my rooms four days [*sic*], and his enemies must have reckoned that he had confided in me. So I would be the next to go. It might be that very night, or next day, or the day after, but my number was up all right" (*TNS* 19). As Hannay leaves his apartment block he observes: "I caught sight of a policeman a hundred yards down, and a loafer shuffling past on the other side. Some impulse made me raise my eyes to the house opposite, and there at a first-floor window was a face. As the loafer passed he looked up, and I fancied a signal was exchanged" (*TNS* 23-4). In the absence of any definitive proof that Scudder's offing was in fact conspiratorially-organized, Hannay's mind goes about the business of interpreting the former's death in accordance with a larger purpose, a purpose in which Hannay is now a key player. This mindset culminates in the moment of critical paranoid vanity, when the paranoiac convinces himself of his own importance. "Here was I,

[11] *Ibid.*, 16.
[12] Nicholas Hiley, "Decoding German Spies: British Spy Fiction, 1908-18," in Wesley K. Wark, ed., *Spy Fiction, Spy Films and Real Intelligence* (London: Frank Cass, 1991), 55-79, at 76. I take the list of paranoid characteristics from Robins and Post, *Political Paranoia*, 8-14.

a very ordinary fellow, with no particular brains, and yet I was convinced that somehow I was needed to help this business through—that without me it would all go to blazes" (*TNS* 86).

But just because Hannay seems paranoid doesn't mean they aren't out to get him: there is a conspiracy at work here, and Hannay correctly identifies it from the very beginning.[13] Having put a tablecloth over Scudder's staring white face, Hannay reflects: "I was in the soup—that was pretty clear. Any shadow of a doubt I might have had about the truth of Scudder's tale was now gone. The proof of it was lying under the tablecloth" (*TNS* 19). If Hannay is paranoid in the truest of psychological senses then he is only so in an attenuated form because his perceptions are not delusional. In David Trotter's view this pathology represents "the 'internalization' of paranoia by a young man who thereby renews both himself and a ruling élite which had hitherto been sunk in complacency."[14] What Hannay does, in essence, is to reconstitute his thought patterns in accordance with Scudder's sceptical point of view, a move he makes so fully that it enables him to make *accurate* readings of intrigue. It is a development anticipated in *The Power-House*: "The amazing and almost incredible thing about this story of mine is the way clues kept rolling in unsolicited, and I was to get another from this dull prosecution. I suppose that the explanation is that the world is full of clues to everything, and that if a man's mind is sharp-set on any quest, he happens to notice and take advantage of what otherwise he would miss" (*PH* 39). For Trotter, this skill-set is professional. Paranoia, in this view, is an expertise that reads mess as "evidence in the visible world of an invisible but comprehensive design."[15] For Trotter, what survives in spy fiction is the belief that psychosis "may under certain circumstances prove a progressive force."[16]

One problem with using *The Thirty-Nine Steps* in any reading of professional identity is the unrelenting insistency with which Hannay's activities are typified as *amateurish*. For instance, Hannay works *alone* for much of the book, outside the professional intelligence and police organizations that he has to work so hard to convince that he is correct about the plot he sees forming in his midst. Professions are not absent

---

[13] Another relevant example of this "true" persecution-mania might be the moment in *Huntingtower* when the narrator reports on McCunn's mindset: "Spies, summoned by Dobson's telegram, were, he was convinced, watching his every movement, and he meant to see that they missed nothing" (*H* 80-1). McCunn really is being followed here.

[14] Trotter, *Paranoid Modernism*, 143.

[15] *Ibid.*, 145.

[16] *Ibid.*, 142.

from *The Thirty-Nine Steps*, of course, and they play a vital role. Hannay himself is a qualified engineer, for instance, and it is stated that he has had some practice of code-breaking as an "intelligence-officer at Delagoa Bay during the Boer War" (*TNS* 25). Moreover, the professions give Hannay various opportunities for disguise, such as when he poses as an orator (*TNS* 44) and when he hides as a roadman: "On I went, trundling my loads of stone, with the heavy step of the professional" (*TNS* 52). But amateurism is a fundamental aspect of Hannay's character. For instance, although Hannay ultimately saves the day he is prone to moments of incompetence, especially in the case of car thievery: "I began to see what an ass I had been to steal the car" (*TNS* 40). Chance plays a significant part in Hannay's success, too. He narrowly misses death "by an ace" (*TNS* 42), happens upon unintentional diversions (*TNS* 30), coincidentally runs into an old associate (*TNS* 55), and admits his indebtedness to "pieces of undeserved good fortune" (*TNS* 57). As he puts it elsewhere: "I resolved not to puzzle my head but to take the gifts the gods had provided" (*TNS* 78). Without a doubt, Hannay's victory is in part enabled by outside influences.

In spite of this, there is a sense in which Hannay's amateurism can be read as closer to the professionalism it ostensibly disallows. Reading *The Thirty-Nine Steps* with an eye to the generic history of the spy thriller, it is not hard to detect in Hannay's neophytism an abandoning of certain totemic, gentlemanly principles (such as fair play, honesty, respect for the law) in favour of the professional detachment of the secret agent. In the same way as Leithen *begins* to take on the qualities of the detective in *The Power-House*, Hannay does not *become* a professional spy, but his actions begin to dismantle the values through which prior incarnations of the gentleman amateur had been articulated. Thus, while Hannay's paranoia is obviously beneficial in his own case it is less so in the case of (usually innocent) others: Hannay punches a policeman (*TNS* 40); he observes that "[c]ontrary to general belief, I was not a murderer, but I had become an unholy liar, a shameless impostor, and a highwayman with a marked taste for expensive motor-cars" (*TNS* 56); and, having been cleared of any wrongdoing by the authorities, he attacks Marmaduke Jopley, previously referred to as "an offence to creation" (*TNS* 55), because the latter unexpectedly stops him in the street: "a delay at that moment seemed to me unendurable, and the sight of Marmie's imbecile face was more than I could bear. I let out with my left, and had the satisfaction of seeing him measure his length in the gutter" (*TNS* 87).

These ambiguities over the standing of paranoia in *The Thirty-Nine Steps* are nicely mirrored in Hannay's claim that, in the special context of espionage, paranoia is not pathological so much as it is ludic, game-like, and infantile. By describing his quest as a "crazy game of hide-and-seek" (*TNS* 57), Hannay implies that paranoid reality is a sphere governed by collective rules and achievable outputs. Scudder refers to the conspiracy as a game (*TNS* 12, 37), as does Walter Bullivant (*TNS* 83) and Hannay himself (*TNS* 20). Hannay notes that he has "a head for things like chess and puzzles" (*TNS* 25), a motif reinforced by his chess-playing with Scudder at the start of the book (*TNS* 16). Hannay envisages the prospect of the fugitive life as "a giddy hunt" (*TNS* 20), and at one stage in his getaway through Scotland he observes: "I felt as if I were taking part in a schoolboy game of hare and hounds" (*TNS* 59). Elsewhere, game-playing modulates into sport: the milkman from whom Hannay borrows a uniform as disguise accepts the request as "'a bit of sport'" (*TNS* 23) and while Hannay flees uphill he sees "[a]way down the slope, a couple of miles away, several men were advancing like a row of beaters at a shoot" (*TNS* 49). Of course, the most important instance of sports-play comes at the end of the text in a tennis game that disguises Hannay's enemies. "It was simply impossible to believe that these three hearty fellows were anything but what they seemed—three ordinary, game-playing, suburban Englishmen, wearisome, if you like, but sordidly innocent" (*TNS* 102). When Hannay breaks their camouflage, and thus undermines their dastardly schemes, he proves the extent to which paranoia functions in this text not as psychosis but as competition, not as illness but as winnable cure.

Nonetheless, if paranoia functions as some kind of completable game here it is only so in a very limited sense. If gaming implies rule-bound contest it also connotes triviality, and indeed *The Thirty-Nine Steps* signals this aspect of the "game" of paranoia by restricting its affect to a "small scale" conspiracy within a network of much larger, and more cataclysmic, machinations. In Trotter's view, the cultural work performed by spy fiction "was to imagine a suspiciousness triggered early enough in the game to avert catastrophe."[17] But, as we have already seen, in Buchan's instance this is not quite right. For what *The Thirty-Nine Steps* depicts is a suspiciousness triggered early enough in the game to avert *one* catastrophe (the Black Stone conspiracy) but *too late* to prevent the wider catastrophe of world war. "The first thing I learned was that it was no question of preventing a war. That was coming, as sure as Christmas: had been arranged, said Scudder, ever since February 1912" (*TNS* 38). *The Thirty-Nine Steps* closes with Hannay defeating his enemies but also with the

---

[17] *Ibid.*, 143.

closing recognition that "[t]hree weeks later, as all the world knows, we went to war" (*TNS* 111). The notion of "internalizing" paranoia here receives a partial reprimand that both underlines the retrospective knowingness with which Buchan constructs his tale as a recapitulation of earlier spy novels, and gestures towards possibilities of a global peace that might have been but never came to pass.

What all this seems to imply is that although texts such as *The Thirty-Nine Steps* ambiguously promote a robust male heroism as a protective measure against external threats, it is in some sense—consciously intended or otherwise—an inconclusive gesture. That is, Buchan's use of paranoid imaginaries renders the male heroic mode that his thrillers exploit as self-validating only in that such heroism is acted out within structures which are in the first place inauthentic. That Buchan returned to the indeterminate nature of the thriller form so frequently is surely symptomatic of his view, expressed towards the end of his life, that "[c]ivilisation after all is a kind of conspiracy" (*CO* 128). Buchan's point that "we live in a world where life must be conducted according to rules," conventions that "we must have if we are not to return to the primeval mire" (*CO* 128-9), is perhaps an invocation of the kind of "open conspiracy" sought by H. G. Wells, but it also stands as a double-sided set of beliefs in which scheming becomes an undesirable and inevitable part of social life. *Memory Hold-the-Door* offers a similar perspective. Consider the following passage: "The years of war," Buchan writes, "were like a trough into which I found myself flung, in company with several million others. Life seemed to stand uneasily still, and in no direction was there any prospect" (*MHD* 165). While the emphasis here is on the life-sapping purposelessness and ethical opacity of conflict on an awesomely heightened scale, Buchan's choice of syntax is revealing. In depicting himself as an object dislocated ("flung") against his will into a war over which he had no control he also draws attention to his own lack of intending selfhood, to the lack of a self-agency responsible for that very dislocation. Two consequences follow from this strategy. On the one hand, it reduces individuals to vessels of sourceless affect, thus reinforcing Buchan's impression of the soldier as a "minor cog" in the "operations of a huge impersonal machine which seemed to move with little intelligent purpose" (*MHD* 165). On the other, it implies the terrible possibility of a dark puppet-master surreptitiously plying the strings of war; an unseen, unnameable conspirator, a "secret agent" (in the literal sense of that term) directly influencing the capricious fortunes of civilization itself.

Buchan's fictions, and especially his thrillers, might be broadly characterized as attempts to probe the consequences of such a predicament, one in which the identity and sovereignty of the individual self is perpetually threatened by unseen dangers, and where civilization hangs always in the balance between lawful protection and anarchistic rebellion. G. K. Chesterton's view of the detective novel as a form that, "[b]y dealing with the unsleeping sentinels who guard the outposts of society, tends to remind us that we live in an armed camp, making war with a chaotic world, and that the criminals, the children of chaos, are nothing but the traitors within our gates" with small effort could be applied to Buchan's texts, which return again and again to the interlinked issues of human frailty, civilization and its discontents, heroism in the face of pandemonium, and the brutalities of a world that has all but conquered individual autonomies.[18] At their most perceptive, Buchan's works try to show that whatever solutions might be discovered for these perils are themselves all too often the preludes to new forms of menace and jeopardy. From this perspective, Buchan's closures can be read as closures in advance of new forms of open-endedness, his faith as a marking of hope in a comfortless, increasingly alienated world.

This tension between an indeterminate, disenchanted modernity and a divinity against which it is defined is the principal fault-line running through Buchan's *oeuvre*. It led him to acknowledge "the tyranny of matter" and the appeal of "absolute things—goodness, truth, beauty" (*MHD* 291), to repudiate greed and materialism wherever he found it in favour of an almost Stoic temperance that conceded humanity's inadequacies in the face of a perplexing "beyond." For Buchan this was not, finally, an impasse: "With the recognition of our limitations comes a glimpse of the majesty of the 'Power not ourselves.' Religion is born when we accept the ultimate frustration of mere human effort, and at the same time realise the strength which comes from union with superhuman reality" (*MHD* 291). Fully aware of man's imperfections, Buchan meditatively wrote: "[d]ogmatism gives place to questioning, and questioning in the end to prayer" (*MHD* 293). What better way to describe the trajectory of his life's work? The tendency this quotation evokes—a recurrent desire to unsettle complacency by recourse to scepticism, a scepticism that is in turn displaced by a belief in the irrevocable mystery of human experience— appears in Buchan's work as an inquiry that is itself the prelude to a final form of faith. *Sick Heart River* clearly signals this development, with its shifting of the thriller form into largely untapped spiritual and pensive emphases, but a text like *Memory Hold-the-Door* is equally of note here for its view of a world in which "the quality of our religion is being put to

---

[18] G. K. Chesterton, *The Defendant* (London: Dent, 1901), 161.

the test" (*MHD* 292). Faced for the second time by a global war rooted in a selfish materialism, Buchan concluded that "the challenge with which we are now faced may restore to us that manly humility which alone gives power. It may bring us back to God. In that case our victory is assured. The Faith is an anvil which has worn out many hammers" (*MHD* 292-3).

SELECT BIBLIOGRAPHY

1. Buchan's fictional works, poems, and short story collections (selected). The majority of these are available in numerous editions, including unedited reprints.

Sir Quixote of the Moors (1895)
Scholar Gipsies (1896)
John Burnet of Barns (1898)
Grey Weather (1899)
A Lost Lady of Old Years (1899)
The Half-Hearted (1900)
The Watcher by the Threshold (1902)
A Lodge in the Wilderness (1906)
Prester John (1910)
The Moon Endureth (1912)
"The Power-House" (1913)
Salute to Adventurers (1915)
The Thirty-Nine Steps (1915)
The Power-House (1916)
Greenmantle (1916)
Poems, Scots and English (1917)
Mr Standfast (1919)
with his wife as "Cadmus and Harmonia," *The Island of Sheep* (1919)
The Path of the King (1921)
Huntingtower (1922)
Midwinter (1923)
The Three Hostages (1924)
John Macnab (1925)
The Dancing Floor (1926)
Witch Wood (1927)
The Runagates Club (1928)
The Courts of the Morning (1929)
Castle Gay (1930)
The Blanket of the Dark (1931)
The Gap in the Curtain (1932)
A Prince of the Captivity (1933)

The Free Fishers (1934)
The House of the Four Winds (1935)
The Island of Sheep (1936)
Sick Heart River (1941)
The Long Traverse (1941)
John Buchan's Collected Poems, eds Andrew Lownie and William Milne
   (Aberdeen: Scottish Cultural Press, 1996)

2. Non-fictional works by Buchan (selected).

Sir Walter Raleigh: The Stanhope Essay (1897)
The African Colony (1903)
The Law Relating to the Taxation of Foreign Income (1905)
Some Eighteenth-Century Byways (1908)
Sir Walter Raleigh (1911)
The Marquis of Montrose (1913)
Andrew Jameson, Lord Ardwall (1913)
Nelson's History of the War (1915-19 in 24 volumes)
Britain's War by Land (1915)
The Achievement of France (1915)
The Battle of Jutland (1916)
The British Front in the West (1916)
The Battle of the Somme, First Phase (1916)
The Battle of the Somme, Second Phase (1917)
The Battle Honours of Scotland (1919)
These for Remembrance (1919)
The History of the South African Forces in France (1920)
A History of the Great War (1921-2 in 4 volumes)
A Book of Escapes and Hurried Journeys (1922)
with Henry Newbolt, *Days to Remember* (1923)
The Last Secrets (1923)
Lord Minto (1924)
The Man and the Book (1925)
The History of the Royal Scots Fusiliers (1925)
Homilies and Recreations (1926)
Montrose (1928)
The Kirk in Scotland (1930)
Sir Walter Scott (1932)
Julius Caesar (1932)
Gordon at Khartoum (1934)
Oliver Cromwell (1934)

The King's Grace (1935)
Augustus (1937)
Canadian Occasions (1940)
Memory Hold-the-Door (1940)
Comments and Characters (1940)

3. Books edited by Buchan.

Essays and Apothegms of Francis Lord Bacon (1894)
Musa Piscatrix (1896)
The Compleat Angler (1901)
Great Hours in Sport (1921)
The Nations of Today: Great Britain (1923)
The Northern Muse: An Anthology of Scots Vernacular Poetry (1924)
South Africa (1927)

4. Correspondence

No collected or complete edition of Buchan's letters currently exists. Among other places, Buchan's letters can be accessed at the National Library of Scotland, Edinburgh University Library, and the Douglas Library at Queen's University in Kingston, Ontario, Canada.

5. Bibliography

Blanchard, Robert G., *The First Editions of John Buchan: A Collector's Bibliography* (Hamden, CT: Archon, 1981)
Hillier, Kenneth and Ross, Michael, *The First Editions of John Buchan: A Collector's Illustrated Bibliography – A Complement to Blanchard* (Clapton in Gordano: Avonworld, 2008)

6. Biography

Buchan, William, *John Buchan: A Memoir* (Buchan & Enright, 1982)
Lownie, Andrew, *John Buchan: The Presbyterian Cavalier* (1995) (Pimlico, 2002)
Smith, Janet Adam, *John Buchan: A Biography* (1965) (Oxford: Oxford University Press, 1985)
Tweedsmuir, Susan *et al.*, *John Buchan by his Wife and Friends* (Hodder and Stoughton, 1947)

7. Criticism

The principle outlet for Buchan criticism is the indefatigable *John Buchan Journal* (1980 to present). Individual articles are not listed below. Unless otherwise noted, London is the site of publication. A full listing of Buchan criticism can be found in Macdonald, *CMF* 197-212. What follows represents only a sampling of the Buchan criticism currently available:

Bloom, Clive, ed., *Spy Thrillers: From Buchan to le Carré* (Macmillan, 1990)
Brantlinger, Patrick, *Rule of Darkness: British Literature and Imperialism, 1830-1914* (Ithaca: Cornell University Press, 1988)
Buchan, Anna, *Unforgettable, Unforgotten* (London: Hodder, 1945)
Buchan, William, *The "Wreath'd Trellis": John Buchan the Writer by His Son* (1955) (Special Collections, Douglas Library, Queen's University at Kingston, 1985)
Buitenhuis, Peter, *The Great War of Words: Literature as Propaganda, 1914-1918 and After* (Batsford, 1989)
Cawelti, John G. and Rosenberg, Bruce A., *The Spy Story* (University of Chicago Press, 1987)
Cheyette, Bryan, *Constructions of "the Jew" in English Literature and Society: Racial Representations, 1875-1945*, new edition (Oxford: Oxford University Press, 1995)
Cockburn, Claud, *Bestseller: The Books that Everyone Read, 1900-1939* (1972; Penguin, 1975)
Coroneos, Con, *Space, Conrad, and Modernity* (Oxford: Oxford University Press, 2002)
Craig, Cairns, *The Modern Scottish Novel: Narrative and the National Imagination* (Edinburgh: Edinburgh University Press, 1999)
Craig, Patricia and Mary Cadogan, *The Lady Investigates: Women Detectives and Spies in Fiction* (OUP, 1986)
Daniell, David, *The Interpreter's House: A Critical Reassessment of John Buchan* (Nelson, 1975)
Denning, Michael, *Cover Stories: Narrative and Ideology in the British Spy Thriller* (Routledge and Kegan Paul, 1987)
Hepburn, Allan, *Intrigue: Espionage and Culture* (New Haven: Yale University Press, 2005)
Himmelfarb, Gertrude, *The Moral Imagination: From Edmund Burke to Lionel Trilling* (Chicago: Ivan R. Dee, 2006)
Horsley, Lee, *Fictions of Power in English Literature, 1900-1950* (London: Longman, 1995)

Howarth, Patrick, *Play Up and Play the Game: The Heroes of Popular Fiction* (Eyre Methuen, 1973)

Kestner, Joseph A., *The Edwardian Detective, 1901-1915* (Aldershot: Ashgate, 2000)

Kitzan, Laurence, *Victorian Writers and the Image of Empire: The Rose-Colored Vision* (Westport, CT: Greenwood Press, 2001)

Kruse, Juanita, *John Buchan (1875-1940) and the Idea of Empire* (Lewiston: Edwin Mellen, 1989)

Macdonald, Kate, *John Buchan: A Companion to the Mystery Fiction* (Jefferson, NC: McFarland, 2009)

—. ed., *Reassessing John Buchan: Beyond* The Thirty-Nine Steps (Pickering & Chatto, 2009)

Masters, Anthony, *Literary Agents: The Novelist as Spy* (Oxford: Blackwell, 1987)

Milbank, Alison, *Dante and the Victorians* (Manchester: Manchester University Press, 1998)

Orel, Harold, *Popular Fiction in England, 1914-1918* (University Press of Kentucky, 1992)

Panek, LeRoy L., *The Special Branch: The British Spy Novel, 1890-1980* (Bowling Green University Popular Press, 1981)

Sandison, Alan, *The Wheel of Empire: A Study of the Imperial Idea in Some Late Nineteenth and Early Twentieth-Century Fiction* (Macmillan, 1967)

Satia, Priya, *Spies in Arabia: The Great War and the Cultural Foundations of Britain's Covert Empire in the Middle East* (Oxford: Oxford University Press, 2008)

Stafford, David, *The Silent Game: The Real World of Imaginary Spies* (Viking, 1988)

Trotter, David, *Paranoid Modernism: Literary Experiment, Psychosis, and the Professionalization of English Society* (Oxford: Oxford University Press, 2001)

Usborne, Richard, *Clubland Heroes: A Nostalgic Study of Some Recurrent Characters in the Romantic Fiction of Dornford Yates, John Buchan, and Sapper*, 2nd edn (1953) (Barrie & Jenkins, 1974)

Wark, Wesley K., ed., *Spy Fiction, Spy Films and Real Intelligence* (London: Frank Cass, 1991)

Webb, Paul, *A Buchan Companion: A Guide to the Novels and Short Stories* (Stroud: Alan Sutton, 1994)

.

INDEX